Fighting France

Fighting France

EDITH WHARTON

AMBERLEY

This edition first published 2014

Amberley Publishing
The Hill, Stroud
Gloucestershire, GL5 4EP

www.amberley-books.com

British Library Cataloguing in Publication Data.
A catalogue record for this book is available from the British Library.

ISBN 978 1 4456 4198 0 (print)
ISBN 978 1 4456 4206 2 (ebook)

Typeset in 11pt on 15pt Minion.
Typesetting and Origination by Amberley Publishing.
Printed in the UK.

Contents

THE LOOK OF PARIS

I
AUGUST

On the 30th of July, 1914, motoring north from Poitiers, we had lunched somewhere by the roadside under apple-trees on the edge of a field. Other fields stretched away on our right and left to a border of woodland and a village steeple. All around was noonday quiet, and the sober disciplined landscape which the traveller's memory is apt to evoke as distinctively French. Sometimes, even to accustomed eyes, these ruled-off fields and compact grey villages seem merely flat and tame; at other moments the sensitive imagination sees in every thrifty sod and even furrow the ceaseless vigilant attachment of generations faithful to the soil. The particular bit of landscape before us spoke in all its lines of that attachment. The air seemed full of the long murmur of human effort, the rhythm of oft-repeated tasks, the serenity of the scene smiled away the war rumours which had hung on us since morning.

All day the sky had been banked with thunder-clouds, but by the time we reached Chartres, toward four o'clock, they had rolled away under the horizon, and the town was so saturated with sunlight that to pass into the cathedral was like entering the dense obscurity of a church in Spain. At first all detail was imperceptible; we were in a hollow night. Then, as the shadows gradually thinned and gathered themselves up into pier and vault and ribbing, there burst out of them great sheets and showers of colour. Framed by such depths of darkness, and steeped in a blaze of mid-summer sun, the familiar windows seemed singularly remote and yet overpoweringly vivid. Now they widened into dark-shored pools splashed with sunset, now glittered and menaced like the shields of fighting angels. Some were cataracts of sapphires, others roses dropped from a saint's tunic, others great carven platters strewn with heavenly regalia, others the sails of galleons bound for the Purple Islands; and in the western wall the scattered fires of the rose-window hung like a constellation in an African night. When one dropped one's eyes form these ethereal harmonies, the dark masses of masonry below them, all veiled and muffled in a mist pricked by a few altar lights, seemed to symbolize the life on earth, with its shadows, its heavy distances and its little islands of illusion. All that a great cathedral can be, all the meanings it can express, all the tranquilizing power it can breathe upon the soul, all the richness of detail it can fuse into a large utterance of strength and beauty, the cathedral of Chartres gave us in that perfect hour.

It was sunset when we reached the gates of Paris. Under the heights of St. Cloud and Suresnes the reaches of the Seine trembled with the blue-pink lustre of an early Monet. The Bois lay about us in the stillness of a holiday evening, and the lawns of Bagatelle were as fresh as June. Below the Arc de Triomphe, the Champs Elysees sloped downward in a sun-powdered haze to the mist of fountains and the ethereal obelisk; and the currents of summer life ebbed and flowed with a normal beat under the trees of the radiating avenues. The great city, so made for peace and art and all humanest graces, seemed to lie by her river-side like a princess guarded by the watchful giant of the Eiffel Tower.

The next day the air was thundery with rumours. Nobody believed them, everybody repeated them. War? Of course there couldn't be war! The Cabinets, like naughty children, were again dangling their feet over the edge; but the whole incalculable weight of things-as-they-were, of the daily necessary business of living, continued calmly and convincingly to assert itself against the bandying of diplomatic words. Paris went on steadily about her mid-summer business of feeding, dressing, and amusing the great army of tourists who were the only invaders she had seen for nearly half a century.

All the while, everyone knew that other work was going on also. The whole fabric of the country's seemingly undisturbed routine was threaded with noiseless invisible currents of preparation, the sense of them was in the calm air as the sense of changing weather is in the balminess of a perfect afternoon. Paris counted the minutes till the evening papers came.

They said little or nothing except what everyone was already declaring all over the country. 'We don't want war – *mais it faut que cela finisse!*' 'This kind of thing has got to stop': that was the only phase one heard. If diplomacy could still arrest the war, so much the better: no one in France wanted it. All who spent the first days of August in Paris will testify to the agreement of feeling on that point. But if war had to come, the country, and every heart in it, was ready.

At the dressmaker's, the next morning, the tired fitters were preparing to leave for their usual holiday. They looked pale and anxious – decidedly, there was a new weight of apprehension in the air. And in the rue Royale, at the corner of the Place de la Concorde, a few people had stopped to look at a little strip of white paper against the wall of the Ministere de la Marine. 'General mobilization' they read – and an armed nation knows what that means. But the group about the paper was small and quiet. Passers by read the notice and went on. There were no cheers, no gesticulations: the dramatic sense of the race had already told them that the event was too great to be dramatized. Like a monstrous landslide it had fallen across the path of an orderly laborious nation, disrupting its routine, annihilating its industries, rending families apart, and burying under a heap of senseless ruin the patiently and painfully wrought machinery of civilization...

That evening, in a restaurant of the rue Royale, we sat at a table in one of the open windows, abreast with the street, and saw the strange new crowds stream by. In an instant we were being shown what mobilization was – a huge break in the normal flow of traffic, like the sudden rupture of a dyke. The street was flooded by the torrent of people sweeping past us to the various railway stations. All were on foot, and carrying their luggage; for since dawn every cab and taxi and motor-omnibus had disappeared. The War Office had thrown out its drag-net and caught them all in. The crowd that passed our window was chiefly composed of conscripts, the *mobilisables* of the first day, who were on the way to the station accompanied by their families and friends; but among them were little clusters of bewildered tourists, labouring along with bags and bundles, and watching their luggage pushed before them on hand-carts – puzzled inarticulate waifs caught in the cross-tides racing to a maelstrom.

In the restaurant, the befrogged and red-coated band poured out patriotic music, and the intervals between the courses that so few waiters were left to serve were broken by the ever-recurring obligation to stand up for the Marseillaise, to stand up for God Save the King, to stand up for the Russian National Anthem, to stand up again for the Marseillaise. '*Et dire que ce sont des Hongrois qui jouent tout cela!*' a humourist remarked from the pavement.

As the evening wore on and the crowd about our window thickened, the loiterers outside began to join in the war-songs. '*Allons, debout!*' – and the loyal round begins again. 'La chanson du depart' is a frequent demand; and the chorus of spectators chimes in roundly. A sort of quiet humour was the note of the street. Down the rue Royale, toward the Madeleine, the bands of other restaurants were attracting other throngs, and martial refrains were strung along the

Boulevard like its garlands of arc-lights. It was a night of singing and acclamations, not boisterous, but gallant and determined. It was Paris *badauderie* at its best.

Meanwhile, beyond the fringe of idlers the steady stream of conscripts still poured along. Wives and families trudged beside them, carrying all kinds of odd improvised bags and bundles. The impression disengaging itself from all this superficial confusion was that of a cheerful steadiness of spirit. The faces ceaselessly streaming by were serious but not sad; nor was there any air of bewilderment – the stare of driven cattle. All these lads and young men seemed to know what they were about and why they were about it. The youngest of them looked suddenly grown up and responsible; they understood their stake in the job, and accepted it.

The next day the army of midsummer travel was immobilized to let the other army move. No more wild rushes to the station, no more bribing of concierges, vain quests for invisible cabs, haggard hours of waiting in the queue at Cook's. No train stirred except to carry soldiers, and the civilians who had not bribed and jammed their way into a cranny of the thronged carriages leaving the first night could only creep back through the hot streets to their hotel and wait. Back they went, disappointed yet half-relieved, to the resounding emptiness of porterless halls, waiterless restaurants, motionless lifts: to the queer disjointed life of fashionable hotels suddenly reduced to the intimacies and make-shift of a Latin Quarter *pension*. Meanwhile it was strange to watch the gradual paralysis of the city. As the motors, taxis, cabs and vans had vanished from the streets, so the lively little steamers had left the Seine. The canal-boats too were gone, or lay motionless: loading and unloading had ceased. Every great architectural opening framed an emptiness; all the endless avenues stretched away to desert distances. In the parks and gardens no one raked the paths or trimmed the borders. The fountains slept in their basins, the worried sparrows fluttered unfed, and vague dogs, shaken out of their daily habits, roamed unquietly, looking for familiar eyes. Paris, so intensely conscious yet so strangely entranced, seemed to have had *curare* injected into all her veins.

The next day – the 2nd of August – from the terrace of the Hotel de Crillon one looked down on a first faint stir of returning life. Now and then a taxi-cab or a private motor crossed the Place de la Concorde, carrying soldiers to the stations. Other conscripts, in detachments, tramped by on foot with bags and banners. One detachment stopped before the black-veiled statue of Strasbourg and laid a garland at her feet. In ordinary times this demonstration would at once have attracted a crowd; but at the very moment when it might have been expected to provoke a patriotic outburst it excited no more attention than if one of the soldiers had turned aside to give a penny to a beggar. The people crossing the square did not even stop to look. The meaning of this apparent indifference was obvious. When an armed nation mobilizes, everybody is busy, and busy in a definite and pressing way. It is not only the fighters that mobilize: those who stay behind must do the same. For each French household, for each individual man or

Motor vehicles requisitioned for the French army.

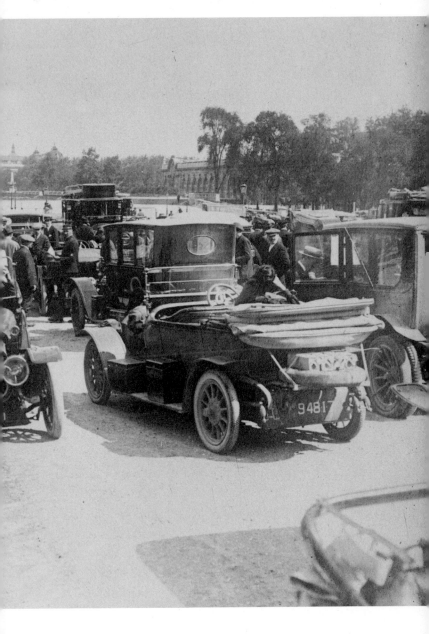

woman in France, war means a complete reorganization of life. The detachment of conscripts, unnoticed, paid their tribute to the Cause and passed on...

Looked back on from these sterner months those early days in Paris, in their setting of grave architecture and summer skies, wear the light of the ideal and the abstract. The sudden flaming up of national life, the abeyance of every small and mean preoccupation, cleared the moral air as the streets had been cleared, and made the spectator feel as though he were reading a great poem on War rather than facing its realities.

Something of this sense of exaltation seemed to penetrate the throngs who streamed up and down the Boulevards till late into the night. All wheeled traffic had ceased, except that of the rare taxi-cabs impressed to carry conscripts to the stations; and the middle of the Boulevards was as thronged with foot-passengers as an Italian market-place on a Sunday morning. The vast tide swayed up and down at a slow pace, breaking now and then to make room for one of the volunteer 'legions' which were forming at every corner: Italian, Roumanian, South American, North American, each headed by its national flag and hailed with cheering as it passed. But even the cheers were sober: Paris was not to be shaken out of her self-imposed serenity. One felt something nobly conscious and voluntary in the mood of this quiet multitude. Yet it was a mixed throng, made up of every class, from the scum of the Exterior Boulevards to the cream of the fashionable restaurants. These people, only two days ago, had been leading a thousand different lives, in indifference or in antagonism to each other, as alien as enemies across a frontier: now workers and idlers, thieves, beggars, saints, poets, drabs and sharpers, genuine people and showy shams, were all bumping up against each other in an instinctive community of emotion. The 'people', luckily, predominated; the faces of workers look best in such a crowd, and there were thousands of them, each illuminated and singled out by its magnesium-flash of passion.

I remember especially the steady-browed faces of the women; and also the small but significant fact that every one of them had remembered to bring her dog. The biggest of these amiable companions had to take their chance of seeing what they could through the forest of human legs; but every one that was portable was snugly lodged in the bend of an elbow, and from this safe perch scores and scores of small serious muzzles, blunt or sharp, smooth or woolly, brown or grey or white or black or brindled, looked out on the scene with the quiet awareness of the Paris dog. It was certainly a good sign that they had not been forgotten that night.

II

WE had been shown, impressively, what it was to live through a mobilization; now we were to learn that mobilization is only one of the concomitants of martial law, and that martial law is not comfortable to live under – at least till one gets used to it.

At first its main purpose, to the neutral civilian, seemed certainly to be the wayward pleasure of complicating his life; and in that line it excelled in the last refinements of ingenuity. Instructions began to shower on us after the lull of the first days: instructions as to what to do, and what not to do, in order to make our presence tolerable and our persons secure. In the first place, foreigners could not remain in France without satisfying the authorities as to their nationality and antecedents; and to do this necessitated repeated ineffective visits to chanceries, consulates and police stations, each too densely thronged with flustered applicants to permit the entrance of one more. Between these vain pilgrimages, the traveller impatient to leave had to toil on foot to distant railway stations, from which he returned baffled by vague answers and disheartened by the declaration that tickets, when achievable, must also be *vises* by the police. There was a moment when it seemed that one's inmost thoughts had to have that unobtainable *visa* – to obtain which, more fruitless hours must be lived on grimy stairways between perspiring layers of fellow-aliens. Meanwhile one's money was probable running short, and one must cable or telegraph for more. Ah – but cables and telegrams must be *vises* too – and even when they were, one got no guarantee that they would be sent! Then one could not use code addresses, and the ridiculous number of words contained in a New York address seemed to multiply as the francs in one's pockets diminished. And when the cable was finally dispatched it was either lost on the way, or reached its destination only to call forth, after anxious days, the disheartening response: 'Impossible at present. Making every effort.' It is fair to add that, tedious and even irritating as many of these transactions were, they were greatly eased by the sudden uniform good-nature of the French functionary, who, for the first time, probably, in the long tradition of his line, broke through its fundamental rule and was kind.

Luckily, too, these incessant comings and goings involved much walking of the beautiful idle summer streets, which grew idler and more beautiful each day. Never had such blue-grey softness of afternoon brooded over Paris, such sunsets turned the heights of the Trocadero into Dido's Carthage, never, above all, so rich a moon ripened through such perfect evenings. The Seine itself had no small share in this mysterious increase of the city's beauty. Released from all traffic, its hurried ripples smoothed themselves into long silken reaches in which quays and monuments at last saw their unbroken images. At night the fire-fly lights of the boats had vanished, and the reflections of the street lamps were lengthened into streamers of red and gold and purple that slept on the calm current like fluted water-weeds. Then the moon rose and took possession of the city, purifying it of all accidents, calming and enlarging it and giving it back its ideal lines of strength and repose. There was something strangely moving in this new Paris of the August evenings, so exposed yet so serene, as though her very beauty shielded her.

So, gradually, we fell into the habit of living under martial law. After the first days of flustered adjustment the personal inconveniences were so few that one felt almost ashamed of their not being more, of not being called on to contribute some greater sacrifice of comfort to the Cause. Within the first week over two thirds of the shops had closed – the greater number bearing on their shuttered windows the notice 'Pour cause de mobilisation', which showed that the 'patron' and staff were at the front. But enough remained open to satisfy every ordinary want, and the closing of the others served to prove how much one could do without. Provisions were as cheap and plentiful as ever, though for a while it was easier to buy food than to have it cooked. The restaurants were closing rapidly, and one often had to wander a long way for a meal, and wait a longer time to get it. A few hotels still carried on a halting life, galvanized by an occasional inrush of travel from Belgium and Germany; but most of them had closed or were being hastily transformed into hospitals.

The signs over these hotel doors first disturbed the dreaming harmony of Paris. In a night, as it seemed, the whole city was hung with Red Crosses. Every other building showed the red and white band across its front, with 'Ouvroir' or 'Hopital' beneath; there was something sinister in these preparations for horrors in which one could not yet believe, in the making of bandages for limbs yet sound and whole, the spreading of pillows for heads yet carried high. But insist as they would on the woe to come, these warning signs did not deeply stir the trance of Paris. The first days of the war were full of a kind of unrealizing confidence, not boastful or fatuous, yet as different as possible from the clear-headed tenacity of purpose that the experience of

ARMÉE DE TERRE ET ARMÉE DE MER

ORDRE
DE MOBILISATION GÉNÉRALE

Par décret du Président de la République, la mobilisation des armées de terre et de mer est ordonnée, ainsi que la réquisition des animaux, voitures et harnais nécessaires au complément de ces armées.

Le premier jour de la mobilisation est le *Dimanche 2 Août*

Tout Français soumis aux obligations militaires doit, sous peine d'être puni avec toute la rigueur des lois, obéir aux prescriptions du **FASCICULE DE MOBILISATION** (pages coloriées placées dans son livret).

Sont visés par le présent ordre **TOUS LES HOMMES** non présents sous les Drapeaux et appartenant :

1° à l'**ARMÉE DE TERRE** y compris les **TROUPES COLONIALES** et les hommes des **SERVICES AUXILIAIRES**;

2° à l'**ARMÉE DE MER** y compris les **INSCRITS MARITIMES** et les **ARMURIERS** de la **MARINE**.

Les Autorités civiles et militaires sont responsables de l'exécution du présent décret.

Le Ministre de la Guerre.　　　　　　　　　　　　*Le Ministre de la Marine.*

Ordre de mobilisation.

the next few months was to develop. It is hard to evoke, without seeming to exaggerate it, that the mood of early August: the assurance, the balance, the kind of smiling fatalism with which Paris moved to her task. It is not impossible that the beauty of the season and the silence of the city may have helped to produce this mood. War, the shrieking fury, had announced herself by a great wave of stillness. Never was desert hush more complete: the silence of a street is always so much deeper than the silence of wood or field.

The heaviness of the August air intensified this impression of suspended life. The days were dumb enough; but at night the hush became acute. In the quarter I inhabit, always deserted in summer, the shuttered streets were mute as catacombs, and the faintest pin-prick of noise seemed to tear a rent in a black pall of silence. I could hear the tired tap of a lame hoof half a mile away, and the tread of the policeman guarding the Embassy across the street beat against the pavement like a series of detonations. Even the variegated noises of the city's waking-up had ceased. If any sweepers, scavengers or rag-pickers still plied their trades they did it as secretly as ghosts. I remember one morning being roused out of a deep sleep by a sudden explosion of noise in my room. I sat up with a start, and found I had been waked by a low-voiced exchange of 'Bonjour's in the street...

Another fact that kept the reality of war from Paris was the curious absence of troops in the streets. After the first rush of conscripts hurrying to their military bases it might have been imagined that the reign of peace had set in. While smaller cities were swarming with soldiers no glitter of arms was reflected in the empty avenues of the capital, no military music sounded through them. Paris scorned all show of war, and fed the patriotism of her children on the mere sight of her beauty. It was enough.

Even when the news of the first ephemeral successes in Alsace began to come in, the Parisians did not swerve from their even gait. The newsboys did all the shouting – and even theirs was presently silenced by decree. It seemed as though it had been unanimously, instinctively decided that the Paris of 1914 should in no respect resemble the Paris of 1870, and as though this resolution had passed at birth into the blood of millions born since that fatal date, and ignorant of its bitter lesson. The unanimity of self-restraint was the notable characteristic of this people suddenly plunged into an unsought and unexpected war. At first their steadiness of spirit might have passed for the bewilderment of a generation born and bred in peace, which did not yet understand what war implied. But it is precisely on such a mood that easy triumphs might have been supposed to have the most disturbing effect. It was the crowd in the street that shouted 'A Berlin!' in 1870; now the crowd in the street continued to mind its own business, in spite of showers of extras and too-sanguine bulletins.

I remember the morning when our butcher's boy brought the news that the first German flag had been hung out on the balcony of the Ministry of War. Now I thought, the Latin will boil over! And I wanted to be there to see. I hurried down the quiet rue de Martignac, turned the corner of the Place Sainte Clotilde, and came on an orderly crowd filling the street before the Ministry of War. The crowd was so orderly that the few pacific gestures of the police easily cleared a way for passing cabs, and for the military motors perpetually dashing up. It was composed of all classes, and there were many family groups, with little boys straddling their mothers' shoulders, or lifted up by the policemen when they were too heavy for their mothers. It is safe to say that there was hardly a man or woman of that crowd who had not a soldier at the front; and there before them hung the enemy's first flag – a splendid silk flag, white and black and crimson, and embroidered in gold. It was the flag of an Alsatian regiment – a regiment of Prussianized Alsace. It symbolized all they most abhorred in the whole abhorrent job that lay ahead of them; it symbolized also their finest ardour and their noblest hate, and the reason why, if every other reason failed, France could never lay down arms till the last of such flags was low. And there they stood and looked at it, not dully or uncomprehendingly, but consciously, advisedly, and in silence; as if already foreseeing all it would cost to keep that flag and add to it others like it; forseeing the cost and accepting it. There seemed to be men's hearts even in the children of that crowd, and in the mothers whose weak arms held them up. So they gazed and went on, and made way for others like them, who gazed in their turn and went on too. All day the crowd renewed itself, and it was always the same crowd, intent and understanding and silent, who looked steadily at the flag, and knew what its being there meant. That, in August, was the look of Paris.

III
FEBRUARY

FEBRUARY dusk on the Seine. The boats are plying again, but they stop at nightfall, and the river is inky-smooth, with the same long weed-like reflections as in August. Only the reflections are fewer and paler; bright lights are muffled everywhere. The line of the quays is scarcely discernible, and the heights of the Trocadero are lost in the blur of night, which presently effaces even the firm tower-tops of Notre-Dame. Down the damp pavements only a few street lamps throw their watery zigzags. The shops are shut, and the windows above them thickly curtained. The faces of the houses are all blind.

In the narrow streets of the Rive Gauche the darkness is even deeper, and the few scattered lights in courts or 'cites' create effects of Piranesi-like mystery. The gleam of the chestnut-roaster's brazier at a street corner deepens the sense of an old adventurous Italy, and the darkness beyond seems full of cloaks and conspiracies. I turn, on my way home, into an empty street between high garden walls, with a single light showing far off at its farther end. Not a soul is in sight between me and that light: my steps echo endlessly in the silence. Presently a dim figure comes around the corner ahead of me. Man or woman? Impossible to tell till I overtake it. The February fog deepens the darkness, and the faces one passes are indistinguishable. As for the numbers of the houses, no one thinks of looking for them. If you know the quarter you count doors from the corner, or try to puzzle out the familiar outline of a balcony or a pediment; if you are in a strange street, you must ask at the nearest tobacconist's – for, as for finding a policeman, a yard off you couldn't tell him from your grandmother!

Such, after six months of war, are the nights of Paris; the days are less remarkable and less romantic.

Almost all the early flush and shiver of romance is gone; or so at least it seems to those who have watched the gradual revival of life. It may appear otherwise to observers from other countries, even from those involved in the war. After London, with all her theaters open, and her machinery of amusement almost unimpaired, Paris no doubt seems like a city on whom great issues weigh. But to those who lived through that first sunlit silent month the streets to-day show an almost normal activity. The vanishing of all the motorbuses, and of the huge lumbering commercial vans, leaves many a forgotten perspective open and reveals many a lost grace of architecture; but the taxi-cabs and private motors are almost as abundant as in peace-time, and the peril of pedestrianism is kept at its normal pitch by the incessant dashing to and fro of those unrivalled engines of destruction, the hospital and War Office motors. Many shops have reopened, a few theatres are tentatively producing patriotic drama or mixed programmes seasonal with sentiment and mirth, and the cinema again unrolls its eventful kilometres.

For a while, in September and October, the streets were made picturesque by the coming and going of English soldiery, and the aggressive flourish of British military motors. Then the fresh faces and smart uniforms disappeared, and now the nearest approach to 'militarism' which Paris offers to the casual sight-seer is the occasional drilling of a handful of *piou-pious* on the muddy reaches of the Place des Invalides. But there is another army in Paris. Its first detachments came months ago, in the dark September days – lamentable rear-guard of the Allies' retreat on Paris. Since then its numbers have grown and grown, its dingy streams have percolated through all the currents of Paris life, so that wherever one goes, in every quarter and at every hour, among the busy confident strongly-stepping Parisians one sees these other people, dazed and slowly moving – men and women with sordid bundles on their backs, shuffling along hesitatingly in their tattered shoes, children dragging at their hands and tired-out babies pressed against their shoulders: the great army of the Refugees. Their faces are unmistakable and unforgettable. No one who has ever caught that stare of dumb bewilderment – or that other look of concentrated horror, full of the reflection of flames and ruins – can shake off the obsession of the Refugees. The look in their eyes is part of the look of Paris. It is the dark shadow on the brightness of the face she turns to the enemy. These poor people cannot look across the borders to eventual triumph. They belong mostly to a class whose knowledge of the world's affairs is measured by the shadow of their village steeple. They are no more curious of the laws of causation than the thousands overwhelmed at Avezzano. They were ploughing and sowing, spinning and weaving and minding their business, when suddenly a great darkness full of fire and blood came down on them. And now they are here, in a strange country, among unfamiliar faces and new ways, with nothing left to them in the world but the memory of burning homes and massacred children and young men dragged to slavery, of infants torn from their mothers, old men trampled by drunken heels and priests slain while they prayed beside the dying. These are the people who stand in hundreds every day outside the doors of the shelters improvised to rescue them, and who receive, in return for the loss of everything that makes life sweet, or intelligible, or at least endurable, a cot in a dormitory, a meal-ticket – and perhaps, on lucky days, a pair of shoes...

Belgian refugees in Paris.

What are the Parisians doing meanwhile? For one thing – and the sign is a good one – they are refilling the shops, and especially, of course, the great 'department stores'. In the early war days there was no stranger sight than those deserted palaces, where one strayed between miles of unpurchased wares in quest of vanished salesmen. A few clerks, of course, were left: enough, one would have thought, for the rare purchasers who disturbed their meditations. But the few there were did not care to be disturbed: they lurked behind their walls of sheeting, their bastions of flannelette, as if ashamed to be discovered. And when one had coaxed them out they went through the necessary gestures automatically, as if mournfully wondering that any one should care to buy. I remember once, at the Louvre, seeing the whole force of a 'department', including the salesman I was trying to cajole into showing me some medicated gauze, desert their posts simultaneously to gather about a motor-cyclist in a muddy uniform who had dropped in to see his pals with tales from the front. But after six months the pressure of normal appetites has begun to reassert itself – and to shop is one of the normal appetites of woman. I say 'shop' instead of buy, to distinguish between the dull purchase of necessities and the voluptuousness of acquiring things one might do without. It is evident that many of the thousands now fighting their way into the great shops must be indulging in the latter delight. At a moment when real wants are reduced to a minimum, how else account for the congestion of the department store? Even allowing for the immense, the perpetual buying of supplies for hospitals and work-rooms, the incessant stoking-up of the innumerable centres of charitable production, there is no explanation of the crowding of the other departments except the fact that woman, however valiant, however tried, however suffering and however self-denying, must eventually, in the long run, and at whatever cost to her pocket and her ideals, begin to shop again. She has renounced the theatre, she denies herself the tea-rooms, she goes apologetically and furtively (and economically) to concerts – but the swinging doors of the department stores suck her irresistibly into their quicksand of remnants and reductions.

No one, in this respect, would wish the look of Paris to be changed. It is a good sign to see the crowds pouring into the shops again, even though the sight is less interesting than that of the other crowds streaming daily – and on Sunday in immensely augmented numbers – across the Pont Alexandre III to the great court of the Invalides where the German trophies are displayed. Here the heart of France beats with a richer blood, and something of its glow passes into foreign veins as one watches the perpetually renewed throngs face to face with the long triple row of German guns. There are few in those throngs to whom one of the deadly pack has not dealt a blow; there are personal losses, lacerating memories, bound up with the sight of all those evil engines. But personal sorrow is the sentiment least visible in the look of Paris. It is not fanciful to say that the Parisian face, after six months of trial, has acquired a new character. The change seems to have affected the very stuff it is moulded of, as though the long ordeal had hardened the poor human clay into some dense commemorative substance. I often pass in the street women whose faces look like memorial medals – idealized images of what they were in the flesh. And the masks of some of the men – those queer tormented Gallic masks, crushed-in and squat and a little satyr-like – look like the bronzes of the Naples Museum, burnt and twisted from their baptism of fire. But none of these faces reveals a personal preoccupation: they are looking, one and all, at France erect on her borders. Even the women who are comparing different widths of Valenciennes at the lace-counter all have something of that vision in their eyes – or else one does not see the ones who haven't.

It is still true of Paris that she has not the air of a capital in arms. There are as few troops to be seen as ever, and but for the coming and going of the orderlies attached to the War Office and the Military Government, and the sprinkling of uniforms about the doors of barracks, there would be no sign of war in the streets – no sign, that is, except the presence of the wounded. It is only lately that they have begun to appear, for in the early months of the war they were not sent to Paris, and the splendidly appointed hospitals of the capital stood almost empty, while others, all over the country, were overcrowded. The motives for the disposal of the wounded have been much speculated upon and variously explained: one of its results may have been the maintaining in Paris of the extraordinary moral health which has given its tone to the whole country, and which is now sound and strong enough to face the sight of any misery.

Parisian fashion in 1914.

And miseries enough it has to face. Day by day the limping figures grow more numerous on the pavement, the pale bandaged heads more frequent in passing carriages. In the stalls at the theatres and concerts there are many uniforms; and their wearers usually have to wait till the hall is emptied before they hobble out on a supporting arm. Most of them are very young, and it is the expression of their faces which I should like to picture and interpret as being the very essence of what I have called the look of Paris. They are grave, these young faces: one hears a great deal of the gaiety in the trenches, but the wounded are not gay. Neither are they sad, however. They are calm, meditative, strangely purified and matured. It is as though their great experience had purged them of pettiness, meanness and frivolity, burning them down to the bare bones of character, the fundamental substance of the soul, and shaping that substance into something so strong and finely tempered that for a long time to come Paris will not care to wear any look unworthy of the look on their faces.

IN ARGONNE

I

The permission to visit a few ambulances and evacuation hospitals behind the lines gave me, at the end of February, my first sight of War.

Paris is no longer included in the military zone, either in fact or in appearance. Though it is still manifestly under the war-cloud, its air of reviving activity produces the illusion that the menace which casts that cloud is far off not only in distance but in time. Paris, a few months ago so alive to the nearness of the enemy, seems to have grown completely oblivious of that nearness; and it is startling, not more than twenty miles from the gates, to pass from such an atmosphere of workaday security to the imminent sense of war.

Going eastward, one begins to feel the change just beyond Meaux. Between that quiet episcopal city and the hill-town of Montmirail, some forty miles farther east, there are no sensational evidences of the great conflict of September – only, here and there, in an unploughed field, or among the fresh brown furrows, a little mound with a wooden cross and a wreath on it. Nevertheless, one begins to perceive, by certain negative signs, that one is already in another world. On the cold February day when we turned out of Meaux and took the road to the Argonne, the change was chiefly shown by the curious absence of life in the villages through which we passed. Now and then a lonely ploughman and his team stood out against the sky, or a child and an old woman looked from a doorway; but many of the fields were fallow and most of the doorways empty. We passed a few carts driven by peasants, a stray wood-cutter in a copse, a road-mender hammering at his stones; but already the 'civilian motor' had disappeared, and all the dust-coloured cars dashing past us were marked with the Red Cross or the number of an army division. At every bridge and railway-crossing a sentinel, standing in the middle of the road with lifted rifle, stopped the motor and examined our papers. In this negative sphere there was hardly any other tangible proof of military rule; but with the descent of the first hill beyond Montmirail there came the positive feeling: *This is war!*

Along the white road rippling away eastward over the dimpled country the army motors were pouring by in endless lines, broken now and then by the dark mass of a tramping regiment or the clatter of a train of artillery. In the intervals between these waves of military traffic we had the road to ourselves, except for the flashing past of despatch-bearers on motor-cycles and of hideously hooting little motors carrying goggled officers in goat-skins and woollen helmets.

The villages along the road all seemed empty – not figuratively but literally empty. None of them has suffered from the German invasion, save by the destruction, here and there, of a single house on which some random malice has wreaked itself; but since the general flight in September all have remained abandoned, or are provisionally occupied by troops, and the rich country between Montmirail and Chalons is a desert.

The first sight of Chame is extraordinarily exhilarating. The old town lying so pleasantly between canal and river is the Head-quarters of an army – not of a corps or of a division, but of a whole army – and the network of grey provincial streets about the Romanesque towers of Notre Dame rustles with the movement of war. The square before the principal hotel – the incomparably named 'Haute Mere-Dieu' – is as vivid a sight as any scene of modern war can be. Rows of grey motor-lorries and omnibuses do not lend themselves to as happy groupings as a detachment of cavalry, and spitting and spurting motor-cycles and 'torpedo' racers are no substitute for the glitter of helmets and the curvetting of chargers; but once the eye has adapted itself to the ugly lines and the neutral tints of the new warfare, the scene in that crowded clattering square becomes positively brilliant. It is a vision of one of the central functions of a great war, in all its concentrated energy, without the saddening suggestions of what, on the distant periphery, that energy is daily and hourly resulting in. Yet even here such suggestions are never long out of sight; for one cannot pass through Chalons without meeting, on their way from the station, a long line of 'eclopes' – the unwounded but battered, shattered, frost-bitten, deafened and half-paralyzed wreckage of the awful struggle. These poor wretches, in their thousands, are daily shipped back from the front to rest and be restored; and it is a grim sight to watch them limping by, and to meet the dazed stare of eyes that have seen what one dare not picture.

If one could think away the 'eclopes' in the streets and the wounded in their hospitals, Chalons would be an invigorating spectacle. When we drove up to the hotel even the grey motors and the sober uniforms seemed to sparkle under the cold sky. The continual coming and going of alert and busy messengers, the riding up of officers (for some still ride!), the arrival of much-decorated military personages in luxurious motors, the hurrying to and fro of orderlies, the perpetual depleting and refilling of the long rows of grey vans across the square, the movements of Red Cross ambulances and the passing of detachments for the front, all these are sights that the pacific stranger could forever gape at. And in the hotel, what a clatter of swords, what a piling up of fur coats and haversacks, what a grouping of bronzed energetic heads about the packed tables in the restaurant! It is not easy for civilians to get to Chalons, and almost every table is occupied by officers and soldiers – for, once off duty, there seems to be no rank distinction in this happy democratic army, and the simple private, if he chooses to treat himself to the excellent fare of the Haute Mere-Dieu, has as good a right to it as his colonel.

The scene in the restaurant is inexhaustibly interesting. The mere attempt to puzzle out the different uniforms is absorbing. A week's experience near the front convinces me that no two uniforms in the French army are alike

A French soldier in the uniform of the period.

either in colour or in cut. Within the last two years the question of colour has greatly preoccupied the French military authorities, who have been seeking an invisible blue; and the range of their experiments is proved by the extraordinary variety of shades of blue, ranging from a sort of greyish robin's-egg to the darkest navy, in which the army is clothed. The result attained is the conviction that no blue is really inconspicuous, and that some of the harsh new slaty tints are no less striking than the deeper shades they have superseded. But to this scale of experimental blues, other colours must be added: the poppy-red of the Spahis' tunics, and various other less familiar colours – grey, and a certain greenish khaki – the use of which is due to the fact that the cloth supply has given out and that all available materials are employed. As for the differences in cut, the uniforms vary from the old tight tunic to the loose belted jacket copied from the English, and the emblems of the various arms and ranks embroidered on these diversified habits add a new element of perplexity. The aviator's wings, the motorist's wheel, and many of the newer symbols, are easily recognizable – but there are all the other arms, and the doctors and the stretcher-bearers, the sappers and miners, and heaven knows how many more ramifications of this great host which is really all the nation.

The main interest of the scene, however, is that it shows almost as many types as uniforms, and that almost all the types are so good. One begins to understand (if one has failed to before) why the French say of themselves: '*La France est une nation guerriere.*'

War is the greatest of paradoxes: the most senseless and disheartening of human retrogressions, and yet the stimulant of qualities of soul which, in every race, can seemingly find no other means of renewal. Everything depends, therefore, on the category of impulses that war excites in a people. Looking at the faces at Chalons, one sees at once in which sense the French are 'une nation guerriere'. It is not too much to say that war has given beauty to faces that were interesting, humorous, acute, malicious, a hundred vivid and expressive things, but last and least of all beautiful. Almost all the faces about these crowded tables – young or old, plain or handsome, distinguished or average – have the same look of quiet authority: it is as though all 'nervosity', fussiness, little personal oddities, meannesses and vulgarities, had been burnt away in a great flame of self-dedication. It is a wonderful example of the rapidity with which purpose models the human countenance. More than half of these men were probably doing dull or useless or unimportant things till the first of last August; now each one of them, however small his job, is sharing in a great task, and knows it, and has been made over by knowing it.

Our road on leaving Chalons continued to run northeastward toward the hills of the Argonne.

We passed through more deserted villages, with soldiers lounging in the doors where old women should have sat with their distaffs, soldiers watering their horses in the village pond, soldiers cooking over gypsy fires in the farm-yards. In the patches of woodland along the road we came upon more soldiers, cutting down pine saplings, chopping them into even lengths and loading them on hand-carts, with the green boughs piled on top. We soon saw to what use they were put, for at every cross-road or railway bridge a warm sentry-box of mud and straw and plaited pine-branches was plastered against a bank or tucked like a swallow's nest into a sheltered corner. A little farther on we began to come more and more frequently on big colonies of 'Seventy-fives'. Drawn up nose to nose, usually against a curtain of woodland, in a field at some distance from the road, and always attended by a cumbrous drove of motor-vans, they looked like giant gazelles feeding among elephants; and the stables of woven pine-boughs which stood nearby might have been the huge huts of their herdsmen.

The country between Marne and Meuse is one of the regions on which German fury spent itself most bestially during the abominable September days. Half way between Chalons and Sainte Menehould we came on the first evidence of the invasion: the lamentable ruins of the village of Auve. These pleasant villages of the Aisne, with their one long street, their half-timbered houses and high-roofed granaries with espaliered gable-ends, are all much of one pattern, and one can easily picture what Auve must have been as it looked out, in the blue September weather, above the ripening pears of its gardens to the crops in the valley and the large landscape beyond. Now it is a mere waste of rubble and cinders, not one threshold distinguishable from another. We saw many other ruined villages after Auve, but this was the first, and perhaps for that reason one

A 'Seventy-five' gun in use.

had there, most hauntingly, the vision of all the separate terrors, anguishes, uprootings and rendings apart involved in the destruction of the obscurest of human communities. The photographs on the walls, the twigs of withered box above the crucifixes, the old wedding-dresses in brass-clamped trunks, the bundles of letters laboriously written and as painfully deciphered, all the thousand and one bits of the past that give meaning and continuity to the present – of all that accumulated warmth nothing was left but a brick-heap and some twisted stove-pipes!

As we ran on toward Sainte Menehould the names on our map showed us that, just beyond the parallel range of hills six or seven miles to the north, the two armies lay interlocked. But we heard no cannon yet, and the first visible evidence of the nearness of the struggle was the encounter, at a bend of the road, of a long line of grey-coated figures tramping toward us between the bayonets of their captors. They were a sturdy lot, this fresh 'bag' from the hills, of a fine fighting age, and much less famished and war-worn than one could have wished. Their broad blond faces were meaningless, guarded, but neither defiant nor unhappy: they seemed none too sorry for their fate.

Our pass from the General Head-quarters carried us to Sainte Menehould on the edge of the Argonne, where we had to apply to the Head-quarters of the division for a farther extension. The Staff are lodged in a house considerably the worse for German occupancy, where offices have been improvised by means of wooden hoardings, and where, sitting in a bare passage on a frayed damask sofa surmounted by theatrical posters and faced by a bed with a plum-coloured counterpane, we listened for a while to the jingle of telephones, the rat-tat of typewriters, the steady hum of dictation and the coming and going of hurried despatch-bearers and orderlies. The extension to the permit was presently delivered with the courteous request that we should push on to Verdun as fast as possible, as civilian motors were not wanted on the road that afternoon; and this request, coupled with the evident stir of activity at Head-quarters, gave us the impression that there must be a good deal happening beyond the low line of hills to the north. How much there was we were soon to know.

We left Sainte Menehould at about eleven, and before twelve o'clock we were nearing a large village on a ridge from which the land swept away to right and left in ample reaches. The first glimpse of the outlying houses showed nothing unusual; but presently the main street turned and dipped downward, and below and beyond us lay a long stretch of ruins: the calcined remains of Clermont-en-Argonne, destroyed by the Germans on the 4th of September. The free and lofty situation of the little town – for it was really a good deal more than a village – makes its present state the more lamentable. One can see it from so far off, and through the torn traceries of its ruined church the eye travels over so lovely a stretch of country! No doubt its beauty enriched the joy of wrecking it.

At the farther end of what was once the main street another small knot of houses has survived. Chief among

them is the Hospice for old men, where Sister Gabrielle
Rosnet, when the authorities of Clermont took to their
heels, stayed behind to defend her charges, and where,
ever since, she has nursed an undiminishing stream
of wounded from the eastern front. We found Soeur
Rosnet, with her Sisters, preparing the midday meal
of her patients in the little kitchen of the Hospice: the
kitchen which is also her dining-room and private
office. She insisted on our finding time to share the
filet and fried potatoes that were just being taken off
the stove, and while we lunched she told us the story
of the invasion – of the Hospice doors broken down 'a
coups de crosse' and the grey officers bursting in with
revolvers, and finding her there before them, in the
big vaulted vestibule, 'alone with my old men and my
Sisters.' Soeur Gabrielle Rosnet is a small round active
woman, with a shrewd and ruddy face of the type that
looks out calmly from the dark background of certain
Flemish pictures. Her blue eyes are full of warmth and
humour, and she puts as much gaiety as wrath into her
tale. She does not spare epithets in talking of 'ces satanes
Allemands' – these Sisters and nurses of the front have
seen sights to dry up the last drop of sentimental pity
– but through all the horror of those fierce September
days, with Clermont blazing about her and the helpless
remnant of its inhabitants under the perpetual threat of
massacre, she retained her sense of the little inevitable
absurdities of life, such as her not knowing how to
address the officer in command 'because he was so tall
that I couldn't see up to his shoulder-straps'. – 'Et ils
etaient tous comme ca,' she added, a sort of reluctant

admiration in her eyes.

A subordinate 'good Sister' had just cleared the table and poured out our coffee when a woman came in to say, in a matter-of-fact tone, that there was hard fighting going on across the valley. She added calmly, as she dipped our plates into a tub, that an obus had just fallen a mile or two off, and that if we liked we could see the fighting from a garden over the way. It did not take us long to reach that garden! Soeur Gabrielle showed the way, bouncing up the stairs of a house across the street, and flying at her heels we came out on a grassy terrace full of soldiers.

The cannon were booming without a pause, and seemingly so near that it was bewildering to look out across empty fields at a hillside that seemed like any other. But luckily somebody had a field-glass, and with its help a little corner of the battle of Vauquois was suddenly brought close to us – the rush of French infantry up the slopes, the feathery drift of French gun-smoke lower down, and, high up, on the wooded crest along the sky, the red lightnings and white puffs of the German artillery. Rap, rap, rap, went the answering guns, as the troops swept up and disappeared into the fire-tongued wood; and we stood there dumbfounded at the accident of having stumbled on this visible episode of the great subterranean struggle.

Though Soeur Rosnet had seen too many such sights to be much moved, she was full of a lively curiosity, and stood beside us, squarely planted in the mud, holding the field-glass to her eyes, or passing it laughingly about among the soldiers. But as we turned to go she said:

'They've sent us word to be ready for another four hundred to-night'; and the twinkle died out of her good eyes.

Her expectations were to be dreadfully surpassed; for, as we learned a fortnight later from a three column *communique,* the scene we had assisted at was no less than the first act of the successful assault on the high-perched village of Vauquois, a point of the first importance to the Germans, since it masked their operations to the north of Varennes and commanded the railway by which, since September, they have been revictualling and reinforcing their army in the Argonne. Vauquois had been taken by them at the end of September and, thanks to its strong position on a rocky spur, had been almost impregnably fortified; but the attack we looked on at from the garden of Clermont, on Sunday, February 28th, carried the victorious French troops to the top of the ridge, and made them masters of a part of the village. Driven from it again that night, they were to retake it after a five days' struggle of exceptional violence and prodigal heroism, and are now securely established there in a position described as 'of vital importance to the operations'. 'But what it cost!' Soeur Gabrielle said, when we saw her again a few days later.

II

The time had come to remember our promise and hurry away from Clermont; but a few miles farther our

French nurses.

attention was arrested by the sight of the Red Cross over a village house. The house was little more than a hovel, the village – Blercourt it was called – a mere hamlet of scattered cottages and cow-stables: a place so easily overlooked that it seemed likely our supplies might be needed there.

An orderly went to find the *medecin-chef,* and we waded after him through the mud to one after another of the cottages in which, with admirable ingenuity, he had managed to create out of next to nothing the indispensable requirements of a second-line ambulance: sterilizing and disinfecting appliances, a bandage-room, a pharmacy, a well-filled wood-shed, and a clean kitchen in which 'tisanes' were brewing over a cheerful fire. A detachment of cavalry was quartered in the village, which the trampling of hoofs had turned into a great morass, and as we picked our way from cottage to cottage in the doctor's wake he told us of the expedients to which he had been put to secure even the few hovels into which his patients were crowded. It was a complaint we were often to hear repeated along this line of the front, where troops and wounded are packed in thousands into villages meant to house four or five hundred; and we admired the skill and devotion with which he had dealt with the difficulty, and managed to lodge his patients decently.

We came back to the high-road, and he asked us if we should like to see the church. It was about three o'clock, and in the low porch the cure was ringing the bell for vespers. We pushed open the inner doors and went in. The church was without aisles, and down the nave stood four rows of wooden cots with brown blankets. In almost every one lay a soldier – the doctor's 'worst cases' – few of them wounded, the greater number stricken with fever, bronchitis, frost-bite, pleurisy, or some other form of trench-sickness too severe to permit of their being carried farther from the front. One or two heads turned on the pillows as we entered, but for the most part the men did not move.

The cure, meanwhile, passing around to the sacristy, had come out before the altar in his vestments, followed by a little white acolyte. A handful of women, probably the only 'civil' inhabitants left, and some of the soldiers we had seen about the village, had entered the church and stood together between the rows of cots; and the service began. It was a sunless afternoon, and the picture was all in monastic shades of black and white and ashen grey: the sick under their earth-coloured blankets, their livid faces against the pillows, the black dresses of the women (they seemed all to be in mourning) and the silver haze floating out from the little acolyte's censer. The only light in the scene – the candle-gleams on the altar, and their reflection in the embroideries of the cure's chasuble – were like a faint streak of sunset on the winter dusk.

For a while the long Latin cadences sounded on through the church; but presently the cure took up in French the Canticle of the Sacred Heart, composed during the war of 1870, and the little congregation joined their trembling voices in the refrain:

Sauvez, sauvez la France,
Ne l'abandonnez pas!

The reiterated appeal rose in a sob above the rows of bodies in the nave: '*Sauvez, sauvez la France,*' the women wailed it near the altar, the soldiers took it up from the door in stronger tones; but the bodies in the cots never stirred, and more and more, as the day faded, the church looked like a quiet grave-yard in a battle-field.

After we had left Sainte Menehould the sense of the nearness and all-pervadingness of the war became even more vivid. Every road branching away to our left was a finger touching a red wound: Varennes, le Four de Paris, le Bois de la Grurie, were not more than eight or ten miles to the north. Along our own road the stream of motor-vans and the trains of ammunition grew longer and more frequent. Once we passed a long line of 'Seventy-fives' going single file up a hillside, farther on we watched a big detachment of artillery galloping across a stretch of open country. The movement of supplies was continuous, and every village through which we passed swarmed with soldiers busy loading or unloading the big vans, or clustered about the commissariat motors while hams and quarters of beef were handed out. As we approached Verdun the cannonade had grown louder again; and when we reached the walls of the town and passed under the iron teeth of the portcullis we felt ourselves in one of the last outposts of a mighty line of defense. The desolation of Verdun is as impressive as the feverish activity of Chalons. The civil population was evacuated in September, and only a small percentage have returned. Nine-tenths of the shops are closed, and as the troops are nearly all in the trenches there is hardly any movement in the streets.

The first duty of the traveller who has successfully passed the challenge of the sentinel at the gates is to climb the steep hill to the citadel at the top of the town. Here the military authorities inspect one's papers, and deliver a 'permis de sejour' which must be verified by the police before lodgings can be obtained. We found the principal hotel much less crowded than the Haute Mere-Dieu at Chalons, though many of the officers of the garrison mess there. The whole atmosphere of the place was different: silent, concentrated, passive.

To the chance observer, Verdun appears to live only in its hospitals; and of these there are fourteen within the walls alone. As darkness fell, the streets became completely deserted, and the cannonade seemed to grow nearer and more incessant. That first night the hush was so intense that every reverberation from the dark hills beyond the walls brought out in the mind its separate vision of destruction; and then, just as the strained imagination could bear no more, the thunder ceased. A moment later, in a court below my windows, a pigeon began to coo; and all night long the two sounds strangely alternated...

On entering the gates, the first sight to attract us had been a colony of roughly-built bungalows scattered over the miry slopes of a little park adjoining the railway station, and surmounted by the sign: 'Evacuation Hospital No. 6.' The next morning we went to visit it. A part of the station buildings has been adapted to hospital use, and among them a great roofless hall, which the surgeon in charge has covered in with canvas and divided down its length into a double row of tents. Each tent contains two wooden cots, scrupulously clean and raised high above the floor; and the immense ward is warmed by a row of stoves down the central passage. In the bungalows across the road are beds for the patients who are to be kept for a time before being transferred to the hospitals in the town. In one bungalow an operating-room has been installed, in another are the bathing arrangements for the newcomers from the trenches. Every possible device for the relief of the wounded has been carefully thought out and intelligently applied by the surgeon in charge and the *infirmiere major* who indefatigably seconds him. Evacuation Hospital No. 6 sprang up in an hour, almost, on the dreadful August day when four thousand wounded lay on stretchers between the railway station and the gate of the little park across the way; and it has gradually grown into the model of what such a hospital may become in skilful and devoted hands.

Verdun has other excellent hospitals for the care of the severely wounded who cannot be sent farther from the front. Among them St. Nicolas, in a big airy building on the Meuse, is an example of a great French Military Hospital at its best; but I visited few others, for the main object of my journey was to get to some of the second-line ambulances beyond the town. The first we went to was in a small village to the north of Verdun, not far from the enemy's lines at Cosenvoye, and was fairly representative of all the others. The dreary muddy village was crammed with troops, and the ambulance had been installed at haphazard in such houses as the military authorities could spare. The arrangements were primitive but clean, and even the dentist had set up his apparatus in one of the rooms. The men lay on mattresses or in wooden cots, and the rooms were heated by stoves. The great need, here as everywhere, was for blankets and clean underclothing; for the wounded are brought in from the front encrusted with frozen mud, and usually without having washed or changed for weeks. There are no women nurses in these second-line ambulances, but all the army doctors we saw seemed intelligent, and anxious to do the best they could for their men in conditions of unusual hardship. The principal obstacle in their way is the over-crowded state of the villages. Thousands of soldiers are camped in all of them, in hygienic conditions that would be bad enough for men in health; and there is also a great need for light diet, since the hospital commissariat of the front apparently supplies no invalid foods, and men burning with fever have to be fed on meat and vegetables.

In the afternoon we started out again in a snow-storm, over a desolate rolling country to the south of Verdun. The wind blew fiercely across the whitened slopes, and no one was in sight but the sentries marching up and down the railway lines, and an occasional cavalryman patrolling the lonely road. Nothing can exceed the mournfulness of this depopulated land: we might have been wandering over the wilds of Poland. We ran some twenty miles down the steel-grey Meuse to a village about four miles west of Les Eparges, the spot where, for weeks past, a desperate struggle had been going on. There must have been a lull in the fighting that day, for the cannon had ceased; but the scene at the point where we left the motor gave us the sense of being on the very edge of the conflict. The long straggling village lay on the river, and the trampling of cavalry and the hauling of guns had turned the land about it into a mud-flat. Before the primitive cottage where the doctor's office had been installed were the motors of the surgeon and the medical inspector who had accompanied us. Nearby stood the usual flock of grey motor-vans, and all about was the coming and going of cavalry remounts, the riding up of officers, the unloading of supplies, the incessant activity of mud-splashed sergeants and men.

The main ambulance was in a grange, of which the two stories had been partitioned off into wards. Under the cobwebby rafters the men lay in rows on clean pallets, and big stoves made the rooms dry and warm. But the great superiority of this ambulance was its nearness to a canalboat which had been fitted up with hot *douches*. The boat was spotlessly clean, and each cabin was shut off by a gay curtain of red-flowered chintz. Those curtains must do almost as much as the hot water to make over the *morale* of the men: they were the most comforting sight of the day.

Farther north, and on the other bank of the Meuse, lies another large village which has been turned into a colony of eclopes. Fifteen hundred sick or exhausted men are housed there – and there are no hot douches or chintz curtains to cheer them! We were taken first to the church, a large featureless building at the head of the street. In the doorway our passage was obstructed by a mountain of damp straw which a gang of hostler-soldiers were pitch-forking out of the aisles. The interior of the church was dim and suffocating. Between the pillars hung screens of plaited straw, forming little enclosures in each of which about a dozen sick men lay on more straw, without mattresses or blankets. No beds, no tables, no chairs, no washing appliances – in their muddy clothes, as they come from the front, they are bedded down on the stone floor like cattle till they are well enough to go back to their job. It was a pitiful contrast to the little church at Blercourt, with the altar lights twinkling above the clean beds; and one wondered if even so near the front, it had to be. 'The African village, we call it,' one of our companions said with a laugh: but the African village has blue sky over it, and a clear stream runs between its mud huts.

We had been told at Sainte Menehould that, for military reasons, we must follow a more southerly direction on our return to Chalons; and when we left Verdun we took the road to Bar-le-Duc. It runs southwest over beautiful broken country, untouched by war except for the fact that its villages, like all the others in this region, are either deserted or occupied by troops. As we left Verdun behind us the sound of the cannon grew fainter and died out, and we had the feeling that we were gradually passing beyond the flaming boundaries into a more normal world; but suddenly, at a cross-road, a sign-post snatched us back to war: *St. Mihiel, 18 Kilometres*. St. Mihiel, the danger-spot of the region, the weak joint in the armour! There it lay, up that harmless-looking bye-road, not much more than ten miles away – a ten minutes' dash would have brought us into the thick of the grey coats and spiked helmets! The shadow of that sign-post followed us for miles, darkening the landscape like the shadow from a racing storm-cloud.

Bar-le-Duc seemed unaware of the cloud. The charming old town was in its normal state of provincial apathy: few soldiers were about, and here at last civilian life again predominated. After a few days on the edge of the war, in that intermediate region under its solemn spell, there is something strangely lowering to the mood in the first sight of a busy unconscious community. One looks instinctively, in the eyes of the passers by, for a reflection of that other vision, and feels diminished by contact with people going so indifferently about their business.

A little way beyond Bar-le-Duc we came on another phase of the war-vision, for our route lay exactly in the track of the August invasion, and between Bar-le-Duc and Vitry-le-Francois the high-road is lined with ruined towns. The first we came to was Laimont, a large village wiped out as if a cyclone had beheaded it; then comes Revigny, a town of over two thousand inhabitants, less completely levelled because its houses were more solidly built, but a spectacle of more tragic desolation, with its wide streets winding between scorched and contorted fragments of masonry, bits of shop-fronts, handsome doorways, the colonnaded court of a public building. A few miles farther lies the most piteous of the group: the village of Heiltz-le-Maurupt, once pleasantly set in gardens and orchards, now an ugly waste like the others, and with a little church so stripped and wounded and dishonoured that it lies there by the roadside like a human victim.

In this part of the country, which is one of many cross-roads, we began to have unexpected difficulty in finding our way, for the names and distances on the milestones have all been effaced, the sign-posts thrown down and the enamelled *plaques* on the houses at the entrance to the villages removed. One report has it that this precaution was taken by the inhabitants at the approach of the invading army, another that the Germans themselves demolished the sign-posts and plastered over the mile-stones in order to paint on them misleading and encouraging distances. The result is extremely bewildering, for, all the villages being either in ruins or uninhabited, there is no one to question but the soldiers one meets, and their answer is almost invariably 'We don't know – we don't belong here.' One is in luck if one comes across a sentinel who knows the name of the village he is guarding.

It was the strangest of sensations to find ourselves in a chartless wilderness within sixty or seventy miles of Paris, and to wander, as we did, for hours across a high heathery waste, with wide blue distances to north and south, and in all the scene not a landmark by means of which we could make a guess at our whereabouts. One of our haphazard turns at last brought us into a muddy bye-road with long lines of 'Seventy-fives' ranged along its banks like grey ant-eaters in some monstrous menagerie. A little farther on we came to a bemired village swarming with artillery and cavalry, and found ourselves in the thick of an encampment just on the move. It seems improbable that we were meant to be there, for our arrival caused such surprise that no sentry remembered to challenge us, and obsequiously saluting *sous-officiers* instantly cleared a way for the motor. So, by a happy accident, we caught one more war-picture, all of vehement movement, as we passed out of the zone of war.

We were still very distinctly in it on returning to Chalons, which, if it had seemed packed on our previous visit, was now quivering and cracking with fresh crowds. The stir about the fountain, in the square before the Haute Mere-Dieu, was more melodramatic than ever. Everyone was in a hurry, every one booted and mudsplashed, and spurred or sworded or despatch-bagged, or somehow labelled as a member of the huge military beehive. The privilege of telephoning and telegraphing being denied to civilians in the war-zone, it was ominous to arrive at night-fall on such a crowded scene, and we were not surprised to be told that there was not a room left at the Haute Mere-Dieu, and that even the sofas in the reading-room had been let for the night. At every other inn in the town we met with the same answer; and finally we decided to ask permission to go on as far as Epernay, about twelve miles off. At Head-quarters we were told that our request could not be granted. No motors are allowed to circulate after night-fall in the zone of war, and the officer charged with the distribution of motor-permits pointed out that, even if an exception were made in our favour, we should probably be turned back by the first sentinel we met, only to find ourselves unable to re-enter Chalons without another permit! This alternative was so alarming that we began to think ourselves relatively lucky to be on the right side of the gates; and we went back to the Haute Mere-Dieu to squeeze into a crowded corner of the restaurant for dinner. The hope that someone might have suddenly left the hotel in the interval was not realized; but after dinner we learned from the landlady that she had certain rooms permanently reserved for the use of the Staff, and that, as these rooms had not yet been called for that evening, we might possibly be allowed to occupy them for the night.

At Chalons the Head-quarters are in the Prefecture, a coldly handsome building of the eighteenth century, and there, in a majestic stone vestibule, beneath the gilded ramp of a great festal staircase, we waited in anxious suspense, among the orderlies and *estafettes*, while our unusual request was considered. The result of the deliberation was an expression of regret: nothing could be done for us, as officers might at any moment arrive from the General Head-quarters and require the rooms. It was then past nine o'clock, and bitterly cold – and we began to wonder. Finally the polite officer who had been charged to dismiss us, moved to compassion at our plight, offered to give us a *laissez-passer* back to Paris. But Paris was about a hundred and twenty-five miles off, the night was dark, the cold was piercing – and at every cross-road and railway crossing a sentinel would have to be convinced of our right to go farther. We remembered the warning given us earlier in the evening, and, declining the offer, went out again into the cold. And just then chance took pity on us. In the restaurant we had run across a friend attached to the Staff, and now, meeting him again in the depth of our difficulty, we were told of lodgings to be found nearby. He could not take us there, for it was past the hour when he had a right to be out, or we either, for that matter, since curfew sounds at nine at Chalons. But he told us how to find our way through the maze of little unlit streets about the Cathedral; standing there beside the motor, in the icy darkness of the deserted square, and whispering hastily, as he turned to leave us: 'You ought not to be out so late; but the word tonight is *Jena.*

The army on the march.

When you give it to the chauffeur, be sure no sentinel overhears you.' With that he was up the wide steps, the glass doors had closed on him, and I stood there in the pitch-black night, suddenly unable to believe that I was I, or Chalons Chalons, or that a young man who in Paris drops in to dine with me and talk over new books and plays, had been whispering a password in my ear to carry me unchallenged to a house a few streets away! The sense of unreality produced by that one word was so overwhelming that for a blissful moment the whole fabric of what I had been experiencing, the whole huge and oppressive and unescapable fact of the war, slipped away like a torn cobweb, and I seemed to see behind it the reassuring face of things as they used to be.

The next morning dispelled that vision. We woke to a noise of guns closer and more incessant than even the first night's cannonade at Verdun; and when we went out into the streets it seemed as if, overnight, a new army had sprung out of the ground. Waylaid at one corner after another by the long tide of troops streaming out through the town to the northern suburbs, we saw in turn all the various divisions of the unfolding frieze: first the infantry and artillery, the sappers and miners, the endless trains of guns and ammunition, then the long line of grey supply-waggons, and finally the stretcher-bearers following the Red Cross ambulances. All the story of a day's warfare was written in the spectacle of that endless silent flow to the front: and we were to read it again, a few days later, in the terse announcement of 'renewed activity' about Suippes, and of the bloody strip of ground gained between Perthes and Beausejour.

IN LORRAINE AND THE VOSGES

NANCY, May 13th, 1915

Beside me, on my writing-table, stands a bunch of peonies, the jolly round-faced pink peonies of the village garden. They were picked this afternoon in the garden of a ruined house at Gerbeviller – a house so calcined and convulsed that, for epithets dire enough to fit it, one would have to borrow from a Hebrew prophet gloating over the fall of a city of idolaters.

Since leaving Paris yesterday we have passed through streets and streets of such murdered houses, through town after town spread out in its last writhings; and before the black holes that were homes, along the edge of the chasms that were streets, everywhere we have seen flowers and vegetables springing up in freshly raked and watered gardens. My pink peonies were not introduced to point the stale allegory of unconscious Nature veiling Man's havoc: they are put on my first page as a symbol of conscious human energy coming back to replant and rebuild the wilderness...

Last March, in the Argonne, the towns we passed through seemed quite dead; but yesterday new life was budding everywhere. We were following another track of the invasion, one of the huge tiger-scratches that the Beast flung over the land last September, between Vitry-le-Francois and Bar-le-Duc. Etrepy, Pargny, Sermaize-les-Bains, Andernay, are the names of this group of victims: Sermaize a pretty watering-place along wooded slopes, the others large villages fringed with farms, and all now mere scrofulous blotches on the soft spring scene. But in many we heard the sound of hammers, and saw brick-layers and masons at work. Even in the most mortally stricken there were signs of returning life: children playing among the stone heaps, and now and then a cautious older face peering out of a shed propped against the ruins. In one place an ancient tram-car had been converted into a cafe and labelled: 'Au Restaurant des Ruines'; and everywhere between the calcined walls the carefully combed gardens aligned their radishes and lettuce-tops.

From Bar-le-Duc we turned northeast, and as we entered the forest of Commercy we began to hear again the Voice of the Front. It was the warmest and stillest of May days, and in the clearing where we stopped for luncheon the familiar boom broke with a magnified loudness on the noonday hush. In the intervals between the crashes there was not a sound but the gnats' hum in the moist sunshine and the dryad-call of the cuckoo from greener depths. At the end of the lane a few cavalrymen rode by in shabby blue, their horses' flanks glinting like ripe chestnuts. They stopped to chat and accept some cigarettes, and when they had trotted off again the gnat, the cuckoo and the cannon took up their trio...

The town of Commercy looked so undisturbed that the cannonade rocking it might have been some unheeded echo of the hills. These frontier towns inured to the clash of war go about their business with what one might call stolidity if there were not finer, and truer, names for it. In Commercy, to be sure, there is little business to go about just now save that connected with the military occupation; but the peaceful look of the sunny sleepy streets made one doubt if the fighting line was really less than five miles away... Yet the French, with an odd perversion of race-vanity, still persist in speaking of themselves as a 'nervous and impressionable' people!

This afternoon, on the road to Gerbeviller, we were again in the track of the September invasion. Over all the slopes now cool with spring foliage the battle rocked backward and forward during those burning autumn days; and every mile of the struggle has left its ghastly traces. The fields are full of wooden crosses which the ploughshare makes a circuit to avoid; many of the villages have been partly wrecked, and here and there an isolated ruin marks the nucleus of a fiercer struggle. But the landscape, in its first sweet leafiness, is so alive with ploughing and sowing and all the natural tasks of spring, that the war scars seem like traces of a long-past woe; and it was not till a bend of the road brought us in sight of Gerbeviller that we breathed again the choking air of present horror.

Gerbeviller, stretched out at ease on its slopes above the Meurthe, must have been a happy place to live in. The streets slanted up between scattered houses

in gardens to the great Louis XIV chateau above the
town and the church that balanced it. So much one can
reconstruct from the first glimpse across the valley; but
when one enters the town all perspective is lost in chaos.
Gerbeviller has taken to herself the title of 'the martyr
town'; an honour to which many sister victims might
dispute her claim! But as a sensational image of havoc
it seems improbable that any can surpass her. Her ruins
seem to have been simultaneously vomited up from the
depths and hurled down from the skies, as though she
had perished in some monstrous clash of earthquake
and tornado; and it fills one with a cold despair to know
that this double destruction was no accident of nature
but a piously planned and methodically executed human
deed. From the opposite heights the poor little garden-
girt town was shelled like a steel fortress; then, when the
Germans entered, a fire was built in every house, and
at the nicely-timed right moment one of the explosive
tabloids which the fearless Teuton carries about for his
land – *Lusitanias* was tossed on each hearth. It was all
so well done that one wonders – almost apologetically
for German thoroughness – that any of the human rats
escaped from their holes; but some did, and were neatly
spitted on lurking bayonets.

One old woman, hearing her son's deathcry, rashly
looked out of her door. A bullet instantly laid her low
among her phloxes and lilies; and there, in her little
garden, her dead body was dishonoured. It seemed
singularly appropriate, in such a scene, to read above
a blackened doorway the sign: 'Monuments Funebres',
and to observe that the house the doorway once

belonged to had formed the angle of a lane called 'La Ruelle des Orphelines'.

At one end of the main street of Gerbeviller there once stood a charming house, of the sober old Lorraine pattern, with low door, deep roof and ample gables: it was in the garden of this house that my pink peonies were picked for me by its owner, Mr. Liegeay, a former Mayor of Gerbeviller, who witnessed all the horrors of the invasion.

Mr. Liegeay is now living in a neighbour's cellar, his own being fully occupied by the debris of his charming house. He told us the story of the three days of the German occupation; how he and his wife and niece, and the niece's babies, took to their cellar while the Germans set the house on fire, and how, peering through a door into the stable-yard, they saw that the soldiers suspected they were within and were trying to get at them. Luckily the incendiaries had heaped wood and straw all round the outside of the house, and the blaze was so hot that they could not reach the door. Between the arch of the doorway and the door itself was a half-moon opening; and Mr. Liegeay and his family, during three days and three nights, broke up all the barrels in the cellar and threw the bits out through the opening to feed the fire in the yard.

Finally, on the third day, when they began to be afraid that the ruins of the house would fall in on them, they made a dash for safety. The house was on the edge of the town, and the women and children managed to get away into the country; but Mr. Liegeay was surprised in his garden by a German soldier. He made a rush for the high wall of the adjoining cemetery, and scrambling over it slipped down between the wall and a big granite cross. The cross was covered with the hideous wire and glass wreaths dear to French mourners; and with these opportune mementoes Mr. Liegeay roofed himself in, lying wedged in his narrow hiding-place from three in the afternoon till night, and listening to the voices of the soldiers who were hunting for him among the grave-stones. Luckily it was their last day at Gerbeviller, and the German retreat saved his life.

Even in Gerbeviller we saw no worse scene of destruction than the particular spot in which the ex-mayor stood while he told his story. He looked about him at the heaps of blackened brick and contorted iron. 'This was my dining-room,' he said. 'There were some good old paneling on the walls, and some fine prints that had been a wedding-present to my grand-father.' He led us into another black pit. 'This was our sitting-room: you see what a view we had.' He sighed, and added philosophically: 'I suppose we were too well off. I even had an electric light out there on the terrace, to read my paper by on summer evenings. Yes, we were too well off...' That was all.

Meanwhile all the town had been red with horror – flame and shot and tortures unnameable; and at the other end of the long street, a woman, a Sister of Charity, had held her own like Soeur Gabrielle at Clermont-en-Argonne, gathering her flock of old men and children about her and interposing her short stout figure between them and the fury of the Germans. We found her in her Hospice, a ruddy, indomitable woman who related with a quiet indignation more thrilling than invective the hideous details of the bloody three days; but that already belongs to the past, and at present she is much more concerned with the task of clothing and feeding Gerbeviller. For two thirds of the population have already 'come home' – that is what they call the return to this desert! 'You see,' Soeur Julie explained, 'there are the crops to sow, the gardens to tend. They had to come back. The government is building wooden shelters for them; and people will surely send us beds and linen.' (Of course they would, one felt as one listened!) 'Heavy boots, too – boots for field-labourers. We want them for women as well as men – like these.' Soeur Julie, smiling, turned up a hob-nailed sole. 'I have directed all the work on our Hospice farm myself. All the women are working in the fields – we must take the place of the men.' And I seemed to see my pink peonies flowering in the very prints of her sturdy boots!

Nancy, the most beautiful town in France, has never been as beautiful as now. Coming back to it last evening from a round of ruins one felt as if the humbler Sisters sacrificed to spare it were pleading with one not to forget them in the contemplation of its dearly-bought perfection.

The last time I looked out on the great architectural setting of the Place Stanislas was on a hot July evening, the evening of the National Fete. The square and the avenues leading to it swarmed with people, and as darkness fell the balanced lines of arches and palaces sprang out in many coloured light. Garlands of lamps looped the arcades leading into the Place de la Carriere, peacock-coloured fires flared from the Arch of Triumph, long curves of radiance beat like wings over the thickets of the park, the sculptures of the fountains, the brown-and-gold foliation of Jean Damour's great gates; and under this roofing of light was the murmur of a happy crowd carelessly celebrating the tradition of half-forgotten victories.

Now, at sunset, all life ceases in Nancy and veil after veil of silence comes down on the deserted Place and its empty perspectives. Last night by nine the few lingering lights in the streets had been put out, every window was blind, and the moonless night lay over the city like a canopy of velvet. Then, from some remote point, the arc of a search-light swept the sky, laid a fugitive pallor on darkened palace-fronts, a gleam of gold on invisible gates, trembled across the black vault and vanished, leaving it still blacker. When we came out of the darkened restaurant on the corner of the square, and the iron curtain of the entrance had been hastily dropped on us, we stood in such complete night that it took a waiter's friendly hand to guide us to the curbstone. Then, as we grew used to the darkness, we saw it lying still more densely under the colonnade of the Place de la Carriere and the clipped trees beyond. The ordered masses of architecture became august, the spaces between them immense, and the black sky faintly strewn with stars seemed to overarch an enchanted city. Not a footstep sounded, not a leaf rustled, not a breath of air drew under the arches. And suddenly, through the dumb night, the sound of the cannon began.

May 14th.

Luncheon with the General Staff in an old bourgeois house of a little town as sleepy as 'Cranford'. In the warm walled gardens everything was blooming at once: laburnums, lilacs, red hawthorn, Banksia roses and all the pleasant border plants that go with box and lavender. Never before did the flowers answer the spring roll-call with such a rush! Upstairs, in the Empire bedroom which the General has turned into his study, it was amusingly incongruous to see the sturdy provincial furniture littered with war-maps, trench-plans, aeroplane photographs and all the documentation of modern war. Through the windows bees hummed, the garden rustled, and one felt, close by, behind the walls of other gardens, the untroubled continuance of a placid and orderly bourgeois life.

We started early for Mousson on the Moselle, the ruined hill-fortress that gives its name to the better-known town at its foot. Our road ran below the long range of the 'Grand Couronne', the line of hills curving southeast from Pont-a-Mousson to St. Nicolas du Port. All through this pleasant broken country the battle shook and swayed last autumn; but few signs of those days are left except the wooden crosses in the fields. No troops are visible, and the pictures of war that made the Argonne so tragic last March are replaced by peaceful rustic scenes. On the way to Mousson the road is overhung by an Italian-looking village clustered about a hill-top. It marks the exact spot at which, last August, the German invasion was finally checked and flung back;

and the Muse of History points out that on this very hill has long stood a memorial shaft inscribed: *Here, in the year 362, Jovinus defeated the Teutonic hordes.*

A little way up the ascent to Mousson we left the motor behind a bit of rising ground. The road is raked by the German lines, and stray pedestrians (unless in a group) are less liable than a motor to have a shell spent on them. We climbed under a driving grey sky which swept gusts of rain across our road. In the lee of the castle we stopped to look down at the valley of the Moselle, the slate roofs of Pont-a-Mousson and the broken bridge which once linked together the two sides of the town. Nothing but the wreck of the bridge showed that we were on the edge of war. The wind was too high for firing, and we saw no reason for believing that the wood just behind the Hospice roof at our feet was seamed with German trenches and bristling with guns, or that from every slope across the valley the eye of the cannon sleeplessly glared. But there the Germans were, drawing an iron ring about three sides of the watch-tower; and as one peered through an embrasure of the ancient walls one gradually found one's self re-living the sensations of the little mediaeval burgh as it looked out on some earlier circle of besiegers. The longer one looked, the more oppressive and menacing the invisibility of the foe became. '*There* they are – and *there* – and *there.*' We strained our eyes obediently, but saw only calm hillsides, dozing farms. It was as if the earth itself were the enemy, as if the hordes of evil were in the clods and grass-blades. Only one conical hill close by showed an odd artificial patterning, like the work of huge ants who had scarred it with criss-cross ridges. We were told that these were French trenches, but they looked much more like the harmless traces of a prehistoric camp.

Suddenly an officer, pointing to the west of the trenched hill said: 'Do you see that farm?' It lay just below, near the river, and so close that good eyes could easily have discerned people or animals in the farm-yard, if there had been any; but the whole place seemed to be sleeping the sleep of bucolic peace. '*They are there,*' the officer said; and the innocent vignette framed by my field-glass suddenly glared back at me like a human mask of hate. The loudest cannonade had not made 'them' seem as real as that!...

At this point the military lines and the old political frontier everywhere overlap, and in a cleft of the wooded hills that conceal the German batteries we saw a dark grey blur on the grey horizon. It was Metz, the Promised City, lying there with its fair steeples and towers, like the mystic banner that Constantine saw upon the sky...

Through wet vineyards and orchards we scrambled down the hill to the river and entered Pont-a-Mousson. It was by mere meteorological good luck that we got there, for if the winds had been asleep the guns would have been awake, and when they wake poor Pont-a-Mousson is not at home to visitors. One understood why as one stood in the riverside garden of the great Premonstratensian Monastery which is now the hospital and the general asylum of the town. Between the clipped limes and formal borders the German shells had scooped out three or four 'dreadful hollows', in one of which, only last week, a little girl found her death; and the facade of the building is pock-marked by shot and disfigured with gaping holes. Yet in this precarious shelter Sister Theresia, of the same indomitable breed as the Sisters of Clermont and Gerbeviller, has gathered a miscellaneous flock of soldiers wounded in the trenches, civilians shattered by the bombardment, eclopes, old women and children: all the human wreckage of this storm-beaten point of the front. Sister Theresia seems in no wise disconcerted by the fact that the shells continually play over her roof. The building is immense

A wounded French soldier is carried to safety.

and spreading, and when one wing is damaged she picks up her protégés and trots them off, bed and baggage, to another. '*Je promene mes malades*,' she said calmly, as if boasting of the varied accommodation of an ultra-modern hospital, as she led us through vaulted and stuccoed galleries where caryatid-saints look down in plaster pomp on the rows of brown-blanketed pallets and the long tables at which haggard eclopes were enjoying their evening soup.

May 15th.

I have seen the happiest being on earth: a man who has found his job.

This afternoon we motored southwest of Nancy to a little place called Menil-sur-Belvitte. The name is not yet intimately known to history, but there are reasons why it deserves to be, and in one man's mind it already is. Menil-sur-Belvitte is a village on the edge of the Vosges. It is badly battered, for awful fighting took place there in the first month of the war. The houses lie in a hollow, and just beyond it the ground rises and spreads into a plateau waving with wheat and backed by wooded slopes – the ideal 'battleground' of the history-books. And here a real above-ground battle of the old obsolete kind took place, and the French, driving the Germans back victoriously, fell by thousands in the trampled wheat.

The church of Menil is a ruin, but the parsonage still stands – a plain little house at the end of the street;

and here the cure received us, and led us into a room which he has turned into a chapel. The chapel is also a war museum, and everything in it has something to do with the battle that took place among the wheat-fields. The candelabra on the altar are made of 'Seventy-five' shells, the Virgin's halo is composed of radiating bayonets, the walls are intricately adorned with German trophies and French relics, and on the ceiling the cure has had painted a kind of zodiacal chart of the whole region, in which Menil-sur-Belvitte's handful of houses figures as the central orb of the system, and Verdun, Nancy, Metz, and Belfort as its humble satellites. But the chapel-museum is only a surplus expression of the cure's impassioned dedication to the dead. His real work has been done on the battle-field, where row after row of graves, marked and listed as soon as the struggle was over, have been fenced about, symmetrically disposed, planted with flowers and young firs, and marked by the names and death-dates of the fallen. As he led us from one of these enclosures to another his face was lit with the flame of a gratified vocation. This particular man was made to do this particular thing: he is a born collector, classifier, and hero-worshipper. In the hall of the 'presbytere' hangs a case of carefully-mounted butterflies, the result, no doubt, of an earlier passion for collecting. His 'specimens' have changed, that is all: he has passed from butterflies to men, from the actual to the visionary Psyche.

On the way to Menil we stopped at the village of Crevic. The Germans were there in August, but the place is untouched – except for one house. That house, a large one, standing in a park at one end of the village, was the birth-place and home of General Lyautey, one of France's best soldiers, and Germany's worst enemy in Africa. It is no exaggeration to say that last August General Lyautey, by his promptness and audacity, saved Morocco for France. The Germans know it, and hate him; and as soon as the first soldiers reached Crevic – so obscure and imperceptible a spot that even German omniscience might have missed it – the officer in command asked for General Lyautey's house, went straight to it, had all the papers, portraits, furniture and family relics piled in a bonfire in the court, and then burnt down the house. As we sat in the neglected park with the plaintive ruin before us we heard from the gardener this typical tale of German thoroughness and German chivalry. It is corroborated by the fact that not another house in Crevic was destroyed.

May 16th.

About two miles from the German frontier (*frontier* just here as well as front) an isolated hill rises out of the Lorraine meadows. East of it, a ribbon of river winds among poplars, and that ribbon is the boundary between Empire and Republic. On such a clear day as this the view from the hill is extraordinarily interesting. From its grassy top a little aeroplane cannon stares to heaven, watching the east for the danger speck; and the circumference of the hill is furrowed by a deep trench – a 'bowel', rather – winding invisibly from one subterranean observation post to another. In each of these earthly warrens (ingeniously wattled, roofed and iron-sheeted) stand two or three artillery officers with keen quiet faces, directing by telephone the fire of batteries nestling somewhere in the woods four or five miles away. Interesting as the place was, the men who lived there interested me far more. They obviously belonged to different classes, and had received a different social education; but their mental and moral fraternity was complete. They were all fairly young, and their faces had the look that war has given to French faces: a look of sharpened intelligence, strengthened will and sobered judgment, as if every faculty, trebly vivified, were so bent on the one end that personal problems had been pushed back to the vanishing point of the great perspective.

From this vigilant height – one of the intentest eyes open on the frontier – we went a short distance down the hillside to a village out of range of the guns, where the commanding officer gave us tea in a charming old house with a terraced garden full of flowers and puppies. Below the terrace, lost Lorraine stretched away to her blue heights, a vision of summer peace: and just above us the unsleeping hill kept watch, its signal-wires trembling night and day. It was one of the intervals of rest and sweetness when the whole horrible black business seems to press most intolerably on the nerves.

Below the village the road wound down to a forest that had formed a dark blur in our bird's-eye view of the plain. We passed into the forest and halted on the edge of a colony of queer exotic huts. On all sides they peeped through the branches, themselves so branched and sodded and leafy that they seemed like some transition form between tree and house. We were in one of the so-called 'villages negres' of the second-line trenches, the jolly little settlements to which the troops retire after doing their shift under fire. This particular colony has been developed to an extreme degree of comfort and safety. The houses are partly underground, connected by deep winding 'bowels' over which light rustic bridges have been thrown, and so profoundly roofed with sods that as much of them as shows above ground is shell-proof. Yet they are real houses, with real doors and windows under their grass-eaves, real furniture inside, and real beds of daisies and pansies at their doors. In the Colonel's bungalow a big bunch of spring flowers bloomed on the table, and everywhere we saw the same neatness and order, the same amused pride in the look of things. The men were dining at long trestle-tables under the trees; tired, unshaven men in shabby uniforms of all cuts and almost every colour. They were off duty, relaxed, in a good humour; but every face had the look of the faces watching on the hill-top. Wherever I go among these men of the front I have the same impression: the impression that the absorbing undivided thought of the Defense of France lives in the heart and brain of each soldier as intensely as in the heart and brain of their chief.

We walked a dozen yards down the road and came to the edge of the forest. A wattled palisade bounded it, and through a gap in the palisade we looked out across a field to the roofs of a quiet village a mile away. I went out a few steps into the field and was abruptly pulled back.

Infantry in the forest.

'Take care – those are the trenches!' What looked like a ridge thrown up by a plough was the enemy's line; and in the quiet village French cannon watched. Suddenly, as we stood there, they woke, and at the same moment we heard the unmistakable Gr-r-r of an aeroplane and saw a Bird of Evil high up against the blue. Snap, snap, snap barked the mitrailleuse on the hill, the soldiers jumped from their wine and strained their eyes through the trees, and the Taube, finding itself the centre of so much attention, turned grey tail and swished away to the concealing clouds.

May 17th.

Today we started with an intenser sense of adventure. Hitherto we had always been told beforehand where we were going and how much we were to be allowed to see; but now we were being launched into the unknown. Beyond a certain point all was conjecture – we knew only that what happened after that would depend on the good-will of a Colonel of Chasseurs-a-pied whom we were to go a long way to find, up into the folds of the mountains on our southeast horizon.

We picked up a staff-officer at Head-quarters and flew on to a battered town on the edge of the hills. From there we wound up through a narrowing valley, under wooded cliffs, to a little settlement where the Colonel of the Brigade was to be found. There was a short conference between the Colonel and our staff-officer, and then we annexed a Captain of Chasseurs and spun away again. Our road lay through a town so exposed that our companion from Head-quarters suggested the advisability of avoiding it; but our guide hadn't the heart to inflict such a disappointment on his new acquaintances. 'Oh, we won't stop the motor – we'll just dash through,' he said indulgently; and in the excess of his indulgence he even permitted us to dash slowly.

Oh, that poor town – when we reached it, along a road ploughed with fresh obus-holes, I didn't want to stop the motor; I wanted to hurry on and blot the picture from my memory! It was doubly sad to look at because of the fact that it wasn't *quite dead*; faint spasms of life still quivered through it. A few children played in the ravaged streets; a few pale mothers watched them from cellar doorways. 'They oughtn't to be here,' our guide explained; 'but about a hundred and fifty begged so hard to stay that the General gave them leave. The officer in command has an eye on them, and whenever he gives the signal they dive down into their burrows. He says they are perfectly obedient. It was he who asked that they might stay...'

Up and up into the hills. The vision of human pain and ruin was lost in beauty. We were among the firs, and the air was full of balm. The mossy banks gave out a scent of rain, and little water-falls from the heights set the branches trembling over secret pools. At each turn of the road, forest, and always more forest, climbing with us as we climbed, and dropped away from us to narrow valleys that converged on slate-blue distances. At one of these turns we overtook a company of soldiers, spade on shoulder and bags of tools across their backs – 'trench-workers' swinging up to the heights to which we were bound. Life must be a better thing in this crystal air than in the mud-welter of the Argonne and the fogs of the North; and these men's faces were fresh with wind and weather.

Higher still ... and presently a halt on a ridge, in another 'black village', this time almost a town! The soldiers gathered round us as the motor stopped – throngs of chasseurs-a-pied in faded, trench-stained uniforms – for few visitors climb to this point, and their pleasure at the sight of new faces was presently expressed in a large '*Vive l'Amerique!*' scrawled on the door of the car. *L'Amerique* was glad and proud to be there, and instantly conscious of breathing an air saturated with courage and the dogged determination to endure. The men were all reservists: that is to say, mostly married, and all beyond the first fighting age. For many months there has not been much active work along this front, no great adventure to rouse the blood and wing the imagination: it has just been month after month of monotonous watching and holding on. And the soldiers' faces showed it: there was no light of heady enterprise in their eyes, but the look of men who knew their job, had thought it over, and were there to hold their bit of France till the day of victory or extermination.

Meanwhile, they had made the best of the situation and turned their quarters into a forest colony that would enchant any normal boy. Their village architecture was more elaborate than any we had yet seen. In the Colonel's 'dugout' a long table decked with lilacs and tulips was spread for tea. In other cheery catacombs we found neat rows of bunks, mess-tables, sizzling sauce-pans over kitchen-fires. Everywhere were endless ingenuities in the way of camp-furniture and household decoration. Farther down the road a path between fir-boughs led to a hidden hospital, a marvel of underground compactness. While we chatted with the surgeon a soldier came in from the trenches: an elderly, bearded man, with a good average civilian face – the kind that one runs against by hundreds in any French crowd. He had a scalp-wound which had just been dressed, and was very pale. The Colonel stopped to ask a few questions, and then, turning to him, said: 'Feeling rather better now?'

'Yes, sir.'

'Good. In a day or two you'll be thinking about going back to the trenches, eh?'

'*I'm going now, sir.*' It was said quite simply, and received in the same way. 'Oh, all right,' the Colonel merely rejoined; but he laid his hand on the man's shoulder as we went out.

Our next visit was to a sod-thatched hut, 'At the sign of the Ambulant Artisans,' where two or three soldiers were modelling and chiselling all kinds of trinkets from the aluminum of enemy shells. One of the ambulant artisans was just finishing a ring with beautifully modelled fauns' heads, another offered me a 'Pickelhaube' small enough for Mustard-seed's wear, but complete in every detail, and inlaid with the bronze eagle from an Imperial pfennig. There are many such ringsmiths among the privates at the front, and the severe, somewhat archaic design of their rings is a proof of the sureness of French taste; but the two we visited happened to be Paris jewellers, for whom 'artisan' was really too modest a pseudonym. Officers and men were evidently proud of their work, and as they stood hammering away in their cramped smithy, a red gleam lighting up the intentness of their faces, they seemed to be beating out the cheerful rhythm of 'I too will something make, and joy in the making.'

Up the hillside, in deeper shadow, was another little structure; a wooden shed with an open gable sheltering an altar with candles and flowers. Here mass is said by one of the conscript priests of the regiment, while his congregation kneel between the fir-trunks, giving life to the old metaphor of the cathedral-forest. Nearby was the grave-yard, where day by day these quiet elderly men lay their comrades, the *peres de famille* who don't go back. The care of this woodland cemetery is left entirely to the soldiers, and they have spent treasures of piety on the inscriptions and decorations of the graves. Fresh flowers are brought up from the valleys to cover them, and when some favourite comrade goes, the men scorning ephemeral tributes, club together to buy a monstrous indestructible wreath with emblazoned streamers. It was near the end of the afternoon, and many soldiers were strolling along the paths between the graves. 'It's their favourite walk at this hour,' the Colonel said. He stopped to look down on a grave smothered in beady tokens, the grave of the last pal to fall. 'He was mentioned in the Order of the Day,' the Colonel explained; and the group of soldiers standing near looked at us proudly, as if sharing their comrade's honour, and wanting to be sure that we understood the reason of their pride...

'And now,' said our Captain of Chasseurs, 'that you've seen the second-line trenches, what do you say to taking a look at the first?'

We followed him to a point higher up the hill, where we plunged into a deep ditch of red earth – the 'bowel' leading to the first lines. It climbed still higher, under the wet firs, and then, turning, dipped over the edge and began to wind in sharp loops down the other side of the ridge. Down we scrambled, single file, our chins on a level with the top of the passage, the close green covert above us. The 'bowel' went twisting down more and more sharply into a deep ravine; and presently, at a

Officers visit the graves of fallen comrades.

bend, we came to a fir-thatched outlook, where a soldier stood with his back to us, his eye glued to a peep-hole in the wattled wall. Another turn, and another outlook; but here it was the iron-rimmed eye of the mitrailleuse that stared across the ravine. By this time we were within a hundred yards or so of the German lines, hidden, like ours, on the other side of the narrowing hollow; and as we stole down and down, the hush and secrecy of the scene, and the sense of that imminent lurking hatred only a few branch-lengths away, seemed to fill the silence with mysterious pulsations. Suddenly a sharp noise broke on them: the rap of a rifle-shot against a tree-trunk a few yards ahead.

'Ah, the sharp-shooter,' said our guide. 'No more talking, please – he's over there, in a tree somewhere, and whenever he hears voices he fires. Some day we shall spot his tree.'

We went on in silence to a point where a few soldiers were sitting on a ledge of rock in a widening of the 'bowel'. They looked as quiet as if they had been waiting for their bocks before a Boulevard cafe.

'Not beyond, please,' said the officer, holding me back; and I stopped.

Here we were, then, actually and literally in the first lines! The knowledge made one's heart tick a little; but, except for another shot or two from our arboreal listener, and the motionless intentness of the soldier's back at the peep-hole, there was nothing to show that we were not a dozen miles away.

Perhaps the thought occurred to our Captain of Chasseurs; for just as I was turning back he said with his friendliest twinkle: 'Do you want awfully to go a little farther? Well, then, come on.'

We went past the soldiers sitting on the ledge and stole down and down, to where the trees ended at the bottom of the ravine. The sharp-shooter had stopped firing, and nothing disturbed the leafy silence but an intermittent drip of rain. We were at the end of the burrow, and the Captain signed to me that I might take a cautious peep round its corner. I looked out and saw a strip of intensely green meadow just under me, and a wooded cliff rising abruptly on its other side. That was all. The wooded cliff swarmed with 'them', and a few steps would have carried us across the interval; yet all about us was silence, and the peace of the forest. Again, for a minute, I had the sense of an all-pervading, invisible power of evil, a saturation of the whole landscape with some hidden vitriol of hate. Then the reaction of the unbelief set in, and I felt myself in a harmless ordinary glen, like a million others on an untroubled earth. We turned and began to climb again, loop by loop, up the 'bowel' – we passed the lolling soldiers, the silent mitrailleuse, we came again to the watcher at his peep-hole. He heard us, let the officer pass, and turned his head with a little sign of understanding.

'Do you want to look down?'

He moved a step away from his window. The look-out projected over the ravine, raking its depths; and here, with one's eye to the leaf-lashed hole, one saw at last ... saw, at the bottom of the harmless glen, half way between cliff and cliff, a grey uniform huddled in a dead heap. 'He's been there for days: they can't fetch him away,' said the watcher, regluing his eye to the hole; and it was almost a relief to find it was after all a tangible enemy hidden over there across the meadow...

The sun had set when we got back to our starting-point in the underground village. The chasseurs-a-pied were lounging along the roadside and standing in gossiping groups about the motor. It was long since they had seen faces from the other life, the life they had left nearly a year earlier and had not been allowed to go back to for a day; and under all their jokes and good-humour their farewell had a tinge of wistfulness. But one felt that this fugitive reminder of a world they had put behind them would pass like a dream, and their minds revert without effort to the one reality: the business of holding their bit of France.

It is hard to say why this sense of the French soldier's single-mindedness is so strong in all who have had even a glimpse of the front; perhaps it is gathered less from what the men say than from the look in their eyes. Even while they are accepting cigarettes and exchanging trench-jokes, the look is there; and when one comes on them unaware it is there also. In the dusk of the forest that look followed us down the mountain; and as we skirted the edge of the ravine between the armies, we felt that on the far side of that dividing line were the men who had made the war, and on the near side the men who had been made by it.

IN THE NORTH

June 19th, 1915.

On the way from Doullens to Montreuil-sur-Mer, on a shining summer afternoon. A road between dusty hedges, choked, literally strangled, by a torrent of westward-streaming troops of all arms. Every few minutes there would come a break in the flow, and our motor would wriggle through, advance a few yards, and be stopped again by a widening of the torrent that jammed us into the ditch and splashed a dazzle of dust into our eyes. The dust was stifling – but through it, what a sight!

Standing up in the car and looking back, we watched the river of war wind toward us. Cavalry, artillery, lancers, infantry, sappers and miners, trench-diggers, road-makers, stretcher-bearers, they swept on as smoothly as if in holiday order. Through the dust, the sun picked out the flash of lances and the gloss of chargers' flanks, flushed rows and rows of determined faces, found the least touch of gold on faded uniforms, silvered the sad grey of mitrailleuses and munition waggons. Close as the men were, they seemed allegorically splendid: as if, under the arch of the sunset, we had been watching the whole French army ride straight into glory...

Finally we left the last detachment behind, and had the country to ourselves. The disfigurement of war has not touched the fields of Artois. The thatched farmhouses dozed in gardens full of roses and hollyhocks, and the hedges above the duck-ponds were weighed down with layers of elder-blossom. On all sides wheat-fields skirted with woodland went billowing away under the breezy light that seemed to carry a breath of the Atlantic on its beams. The road ran up and down as if our motor were a ship on a deep-sea swell; and such a sense of space and light was in the distances, such a veil of beauty over the whole world, that the vision of that army on the move grew more and more fabulous and epic.

The sun had set and the sea-twilight was rolling in when we dipped down from the town of Montreuil to the valley below, where the towers of an ancient abbey-church rise above terraced orchards. The gates at the end of the avenue were thrown open, and the motor drove into a monastery court full of box and roses. Everything was sweet and secluded in this mediaeval place; and from the shadow of cloisters and arched passages groups of nuns fluttered out, nuns all black or all white, gliding, peering and standing at gaze. It was as if we had plunged back into a century to which motors were unknown and our car had been some monster cast up from a Barbary shipwreck; and the startled attitudes of these holy women did credit to their sense of the picturesque; for the Abbey of Neuville is now a great Belgian hospital, and such monsters must frequently intrude on its seclusion...

Sunset, and summer dusk, and the moon. Under the monastery windows a walled garden with stone pavilions at the angles and the drip of a fountain. Below it, tiers of orchard-terraces fading into a great moon-confused plain that might be either fields or sea...

June 20th.

Today our way ran northeast, through a landscape so English that there was no incongruity in the sprinkling of khaki along the road. Even the villages look English: the same plum-red brick of tidy self-respecting houses, neat, demure and freshly painted, the gardens all bursting with flowers, the landscape hedgerowed and willowed and fed with water-courses, the people's faces square and pink and honest, and the signs over the shops in a language half way between English and German. Only the architecture of the towns is French, of a reserved and robust northern type, but unmistakably in the same great tradition.

War still seemed so far off that one had time for these digressions as the motor flew on over the undulating miles. But presently we came on an aviation camp spreading its sheds over a wide plateau. Here the khaki throng was thicker and the familiar military stir enlivened the landscape. A few miles farther, and we found ourselves in what was seemingly a big English town oddly grouped about a nucleus of French churches. This was St. Omer, grey, spacious, coldly clean in its Sunday emptiness. At the street crossings English sentries stood mechanically directing the absent traffic with gestures familiar to Piccadilly; and the signs of the British Red Cross and St. John's Ambulance hung on club-like facades that might almost have claimed a home in Pall Mall.

The Englishness of things was emphasized, as we passed out through the suburbs, by the look of the crowd on the canal bridges and along the roads. Every nation has its own way of loitering, and there is nothing so unlike the French way as the English. Even if all these tall youths had not been in khaki, and the girls with them so pink and countrified, one would instantly have recognized the passive northern way of letting a holiday soak in instead of squeezing out its juices with feverish fingers.

When we turned westward from St. Omer, across the same pastures and watercourses, we were faced by two hills standing up abruptly out of the plain; and on the top of one rose the walls and towers of a compact little mediaeval town. As we took the windings that led up to it a sense of Italy began to penetrate the persistent impression of being somewhere near the English Channel. The town we were approaching might have been a queer dream-blend of Winchelsea and San Gimignano; but when we entered the gates of Cassel we were in a place so intensely itself that all analogies dropped out of mind.

It was not surprising to learn from the guide-book that Cassel has the most extensive view of any town in Europe: one felt at once that it differed in all sorts of marked and self-assertive ways from every other town, and would be almost sure to have the best things going in every line. And the line of an illimitable horizon is exactly the best to set off its own quaint compactness.

We found our hotel in the most perfect of little market squares, with a Renaissance town-hall on one side, and on the other a miniature Spanish palace with a front of rosy brick adorned by grey carvings. The square was crowded with English army motors and beautiful prancing chargers; and the restaurant of the inn (which has the luck to face the pink and grey palace) swarmed with khaki tea-drinkers turning indifferent shoulders to the widest view in Europe. It is one of the most detestable things about war that everything connected with it, except the death and ruin that result, is such a heightening of life, so visually stimulating and absorbing. 'It was gay and terrible,' is the phrase forever recurring in *War and Peace*; and the gaiety of war was everywhere in Cassel, transforming the lifeless little town into a romantic stage-setting full of the flash of arms and the virile animation of young faces.

From the park on top of the hill we looked down on another picture. All about us was the plain, its distant rim merged in northern sea-mist; and through the mist, in the glitter of the afternoon sun, far-off towns and shadowy towers lay steeped, as it seemed, in summer quiet. For a moment, while we looked, the vision of war shrivelled up like a painted veil; then we caught the names pronounced by a group of English soldiers leaning over the parapet at our side. 'That's Dunkerque' – one of them pointed it out with his pipe – 'and there's Poperinghe, just under us; that's Furnes beyond, and Ypres and Dixmude, and Nieuport...' And at the mention of those names the scene grew dark again, and we felt the passing of the Angel to whom was given the Key of the Bottomless Pit.

That night we went up once more to the rock of Cassel. The moon was full, and as civilians are not allowed out alone after dark a staff-officer went with us to show us the view from the roof of the disused Casino on top of the rock. It was the queerest of sensations to push open a glazed door and find ourselves in a spectral painted room with soldiers dozing in the moonlight on polished floors, their kits stacked on the gaming tables. We passed through a big vestibule among more soldiers lounging in the half-light, and up a long staircase to the roof where a watcher challenged us and then let us go to the edge of the parapet. Directly below lay the unlit mass of the town. To the northwest a single sharp hill, the 'Mont des Cats', stood out against the sky; the rest of the horizon was unbroken, and floating in misty moonlight. The outline of the ruined towns had vanished and peace seemed to have won back the world. But as we stood there a red flash started out of the mist far off to the northwest; then another and another flickered up at different points of the long curve. 'Luminous bombs thrown up along the lines,' our guide explained; and just then, at still another point a white light opened like a tropical flower, spread to full bloom and drew itself back into the night. 'A flare,' we were told; and another white flower bloomed out farther down. Below us, the roofs of Cassel slept their provincial sleep, the moonlight picking out every leaf in the gardens; while beyond, those infernal flowers continued to open and shut along the curve of death.

June 21st.

On the road from Cassel to Poperinghe. Heat, dust, crowds, confusion, all the sordid shabby rear-view of war. The road running across the plain between white-powdered hedges was ploughed up by numberless motor-vans, supply-waggons and Red Cross ambulances. Labouring through between them came detachments of British artillery, clattering gun-carriages, straight young figures on glossy horses, long Phidian lines of youths so ingenuously fair that one wondered how they could have looked on the Medusa face of war and lived. Men and beasts, in spite of the dust, were as fresh and sleek as if they had come from a bath; and everywhere along the wayside were improvised camps, with tents made of waggon-covers, where the ceaseless indomitable work of cleaning was being carried out in all its searching details. Shirts were drying on elder-bushes, kettles boiling over gypsy fires, men shaving, blacking their boots, cleaning their guns, rubbing down their horses, greasing their saddles, polishing their stirrups and bits: on all sides a general cheery struggle against the prevailing dust, discomfort and disorder. Here and there a young soldier leaned against a garden paling to talk to a girl among the hollyhocks, or an older soldier initiated a group of children into some mystery of military housekeeping; and everywhere were the same signs of friendly inarticulate understanding with the owners of the fields and gardens.

From the thronged high-road we passed into the emptiness of deserted Poperinghe, and out again on the way to Ypres. Beyond the flats and wind-mills to our left were the invisible German lines, and the staff-officer who was with us leaned forward to caution our chauffeur: 'No tooting between here and Ypres.' There was still a good deal of movement on the road, though it was less crowded with troops than near Poperinghe; but as we passed through the last village and approached the low line of houses ahead, the silence and emptiness widened about us. That low line was Ypres; every monument that marked it, that gave it an individual outline, is gone. It is a town without a profile.

The motor slipped through a suburb of small brick houses and stopped under cover of some slightly taller buildings. Another military motor waited there, the chauffeur relic-hunting in the gutted houses.

We got out and walked toward the centre of the Cloth Market. We had seen evacuated towns – Verdun, Badonviller, Raon-l'Etape – but we had seen no emptiness like this. Not a human being was in the streets. Endless lines of houses looked down on us from vacant windows. Our footsteps echoed like the tramp of a crowd, our lowered voices seemed to shout. In one street we came on three English soldiers who were carrying a piano out of a house and lifting it onto a hand-cart. They stopped to stare at us, and we stared back. It seemed an age since we had seen a living being! One of the soldiers scrambled into the cart and tapped out a tune on the cracked key-board, and we all laughed with relief at the foolish noise... Then we walked on and were alone again.

We had seen other ruined towns, but none like this. The towns of Lorraine were blown up, burnt down, deliberately erased from the earth. At worst they are like stone-yards, at best like Pompeii. But Ypres has been bombarded to death, and the outer walls of its houses are still standing, so that it presents the distant semblance of a living city, while nearby it is seen to be a disembowelled corpse. Every window-pane is smashed, nearly every building unroofed, and some house-fronts are sliced clean off, with the different stories exposed, as if for the stage-setting of a farce. In these exposed interiors the poor little household gods shiver and blink like owls surprised in a hollow tree. A hundred signs of intimate and humble tastes, of humdrum pursuits, of family association, cling to the unmasked walls. Whiskered photographs fade on morning-glory wallpapers, plaster saints pine under glass bells, antimacassars droop from plush sofas, yellowing diplomas display their seals on office walls. It was all so still and familiar that it seemed as if the people for whom these things had a meaning might at any moment come back and take up their daily business. And then – crash! the guns began, slamming out volley after volley all along the English lines, and the poor frail web of things that had made up the lives of a vanished city-full hung dangling before us in that deathly blast.

We had just reached the square before the Cathedral when the cannonade began, and its roar seemed to build a roof of iron over the glorious ruins of Ypres. The singular distinction of the city is that it is destroyed but not abased. The walls of the Cathedral, the long bulk of the Cloth Market, still lift themselves above the market place with a majesty that seems to silence compassion.

The ruins of Ypres.

The sight of those facades, so proud in death, recalled a phrase used soon after the fall of Liege by Belgium's Foreign Minister – '*La Belgique ne regrette rien*' – which ought some day to serve as the motto of the renovated city.

We were turning to go when we heard a whirr overhead, followed by a volley of mitrailleuse. High up in the blue, over the centre of the dead city, flew a German aeroplane; and all about it hundreds of white shrapnel tufts burst out in the summer sky like the miraculous snow-fall of Italian legend. Up and up they flew, on the trail of the Taube, and on flew the Taube, faster still, till quarry and pack were lost in mist, and the barking of the mitrailleuse died out. So we left Ypres to the death-silence in which we had found her.

The afternoon carried us back to Poperinghe, where I was bound on a quest for lace-cushions of the special kind required by our Flemish refugees. The model is unobtainable in France, and I had been told – with few and vague indications – that I might find the cushions in a certain convent of the city. But in which?

Poperinghe, though little injured, is almost empty. In its tidy desolation it looks like a town on which a wicked enchanter has laid a spell. We roamed from quarter to quarter, hunting for someone to show us the way to the convent I was looking for, till at last a passer-by led us to a door which seemed the right one. At our knock the bars were drawn and a cloistered face looked out. No, there were no cushions there; and the nun had never heard of the order we named. But there were the Penitents, the Benedictines – we might try. Our guide offered to show us the way and we went on. From one or two windows, wondering heads looked out and vanished; but the streets were lifeless. At last we came to a convent where there were no nuns left, but where, the caretaker told us, there were cushions – a great many. He led us through pale blue passages, up cold stairs, through rooms that smelt of linen and lavender. We passed a chapel with plaster saints in white niches above paper flowers. Everything was cold and bare and blank: like a mind from which memory has gone. We came to a class room with lines of empty benches facing a blue-mantled Virgin; and here, on the floor, lay rows and rows of lace-cushions. On each a bit of lace had been begun – and there they had been dropped when nuns and pupils fled. They had not been left in disorder: the rows had been laid out evenly, a handkerchief thrown over each cushion. And that orderly arrest of life seemed sadder than any scene of disarray. It symbolized the senseless paralysis of a whole nation's activities. Here were a houseful of women and children, yesterday engaged in a useful task and now aimlessly astray over the earth. And in hundreds of such houses, in dozens, in hundreds of open towns, the hand of time had been stopped, the heart of life had ceased to beat, all the currents of hope and happiness and industry been choked – not that some great military end might be gained, or the length of the war curtailed, but that, wherever the shadow of Germany falls, all things should wither at the root.

The same sight met us everywhere that afternoon. Over Furnes and Bergues, and all the little intermediate villages, the evil shadow lay. Germany had willed that these places should die, and wherever her bombs could not reach her malediction had carried. Only Biblical lamentation can convey a vision of this life-drained land. 'Your country is desolate; your cities are burned with fire; your land, strangers devour it in your presence, and it is desolate, as overthrown by strangers.'

Late in the afternoon we came to Dunkerque, lying peacefully between its harbour and canals. The bombardment of the previous month had emptied it, and though no signs of damage were visible the same spellbound air lay over everything. As we sat alone at tea in the hall of the hotel on the Place Jean Bart, and looked out on the silent square and its lifeless shops and cafes, someone suggested that the hotel would be a convenient centre for the excursions we had planned, and we decided to return there the next evening. Then we motored back to Cassel.

June 22nd.

My first waking thought was: 'How time flies! It must be the Fourteenth of July!' I knew it could not be the Fourth of that specially commemorative month, because I was just awake enough to be sure I was not in America; and the only other event to justify such a terrific clatter was the French national anniversary. I sat up and listened to the popping of guns till a completed sense of reality stole over me, and I realized that I was in the inn of the Wild Man at Cassel, and that it was not the fourteenth of July but the twenty-second of June.

Then, what – ? A Taube, of course! And all the guns in the place were cracking at it! By the time this mental process was complete, I had scrambled up and hurried downstairs and, unbolting the heavy doors, had rushed out into the square. It was about four in the morning, the heavenliest moment of a summer dawn, and in spite of the tumult Cassel still apparently slept. Only a few soldiers stood in the square, looking up at a drift of white cloud behind which – they averred – a Taube had just slipped out of sight. Cassel was evidently used to Taubes, and I had the sense of having overdone my excitement and not being exactly in tune; so after gazing a moment at the white cloud I slunk back into the hotel, barred the door and mounted to my room. At a window on the stairs I paused to look out over the sloping roofs of the town, the gardens, the plain; and suddenly there was another crash and a drift of white smoke blew up from the fruit-trees just under the window. It was a last shot at the fugitive, from a gun hidden in one of those quiet provincial gardens between the houses; and its secret presence there was more startling than all the clatter of mitrailleuses from the rock.

Silence and sleep came down again on Cassel; but an hour or two later the hush was broken by a roar like the last trump. This time it was no question of mitrailleuses. The Wild Man rocked on its base, and every pane in my windows beat a tattoo. What was that incredible unimagined sound? Why, it could be nothing, of course, but the voice of the big siege-gun of Dixmude! Five times, while I was dressing, the thunder shook my windows, and the air was filled with a noise that may be compared – if the human imagination can stand the strain – to the simultaneous closing of all the iron shop-shutters in the world. The odd part was that, as far as the Wild Man and its inhabitants were concerned, no visible effects resulted, and dressing, packing and coffee-drinking went on comfortably in the strange parentheses between the roars.

We set off early for a neighbouring Head-quarters, and it was not till we turned out of the gates of Cassel that we came on signs of the bombardment: the smashing of a gas-house and the converting of a cabbage-field into a crater which, for some time to come, will spare photographers the trouble of climbing Vesuvius. There was a certain consolation in the discrepancy between the noise and the damage done.

At Head-quarters we learned more of the morning's incidents. Dunkerque, it appeared, had first been visited by the Taube which afterward came to take the range of Cassel; and the big gun of Dixmude had then turned all its fury on the French sea-port. The bombardment of Dunkuerque was still going on; and we were asked, and in fact bidden, to give up our plan of going there for the night.

After luncheon we turned north, toward the dunes. The villages we drove through were all evacuated, some quite lifeless, others occupied by troops. Presently we came to a group of military motors drawn up by the roadside, and a field black with wheeling troops. 'Admiral Ronarc'h!' our companion from Head-quarters exclaimed; and we understood that we had had the good luck to come on the hero of Dixmude in the act of reviewing the marine fusiliers and territorials whose magnificent defense of last October gave that much-besieged town another lease of glory.

We stopped the motor and climbed to a ridge above the field. A high wind was blowing, bringing with it the booming of the guns along the front. A sun half-veiled in sand-dust shone on pale meadows, sandy flats, grey wind-mills. The scene was deserted, except for the handful of troops deploying before the officers on the edge of the field. Admiral Ronarc'h, white-gloved and in full-dress uniform, stood a little in advance, a young naval officer at his side. He had just been distributing decorations to his fusiliers and territorials, and they were marching past him, flags flying and bugles playing. Every one of those men had a record of heroism, and every face in those ranks had looked on horrors unnameable. They had lost Dixmude – for a while – but they had gained great glory, and the inspiration of their epic resistance had come from the quiet officer who stood there, straight and grave, in his white gloves and gala uniform.

One must have been in the North to know something of the tie that exists, in this region of bitter and continuous fighting, between officers and soldiers. The feeling of the chiefs is almost one of veneration for their men; that

Remise de décorations par l'Amiral Ronarc'h.

Admiral Ronarc'h carrying out his inspection.

of the soldiers, a kind of half-humorous tenderness for the officers who have faced such odds with them. This mutual regard reveals itself in a hundred undefinable ways; but its fullest expression is in the tone with which the commanding officers speak the two words oftenest on their lips: 'My men.'

The little review over, we went on to Admiral Ronarc'h's quarters in the dunes, and thence, after a brief visit, to another brigade Head-quarters. We were in a region of sandy hillocks feathered by tamarisk, and interspersed with poplar groves slanting like wheat in the wind. Between these meagre thickets the roofs of seaside bungalows showed above the dunes; and before one of these we stopped, and were led into a sitting-room full of maps and aeroplane photographs. One of the officers of the brigade telephoned to ask if the way was clear to Nieuport; and the answer was that we might go on.

Our road ran through the 'Bois Triangulaire', a bit of woodland exposed to constant shelling. Half the poor spindling trees were down, and patches of blackened undergrowth and ragged hollows marked the path of the shells. If the trees of a cannonaded wood are of strong inland growth their fallen trunks have the majesty of a ruined temple; but there was something humanly pitiful in the frail trunks of the Bois Triangulaire, lying there like slaughtered rows of immature troops.

A few miles more brought us to Nieuport, most lamentable of the victim towns. It is not empty as Ypres is empty: troops are quartered in the cellars, and at the approach of our motor knots of cheerful zouaves came swarming out of the ground like ants. But Ypres is majestic in death, poor Nieuport gruesomely comic. About its splendid nucleus of mediaeval architecture a modern town had grown up; and nothing stranger can be pictured than the contrast between the streets of flimsy houses, twisted like curl-papers, and the ruins of the Gothic Cathedral and the Cloth Market. It is like passing from a smashed toy to the survival of a prehistoric cataclysm.

Modern Nieuport seems to have died in a colic. No less homely image expresses the contractions and contortions of the houses reaching out the appeal of their desperate chimney-pots and agonized girders. There is one view along the exterior of the town like nothing else on the warfront. On the left, a line of palsied houses leads up like a string of crutch-propped beggars to the mighty ruin of the Templars' Tower; on the right the flats reach away to the almost imperceptible humps of masonry that were once the villages of St. Georges, Ramscappelle, Pervyse. And over it all the incessant crash of the guns stretches a sounding-board of steel.

In front of the cathedral a German shell has dug a crater thirty feet across, overhung by splintered tree-trunks, burnt shrubs, vague mounds of rubbish; and a few steps beyond lies the peacefullest spot in Nieuport, the grave-yard where the zouaves have buried their comrades. The dead are laid in rows under the flank of the cathedral, and on their carefully set grave-stones have been placed collections of pious images gathered from the ruined houses. Some of the most privileged are guarded by colonies of plaster saints and Virgins that cover the whole slab; and over the handsomest Virgins and the most gaily coloured saints the soldiers have placed the glass bells that once protected the parlour clocks and wedding-wreaths in the same houses.

From sad Nieuport we motored on to a little seaside colony where gaiety prevails. Here the big hotels and the adjoining villas along the beach are filled with troops just back from the trenches: it is one of the 'rest cures' of the front. When we drove up, the regiment 'au repos' was assembled in the wide sandy space between the principal hotels, and in the centre of the jolly crowd the band was playing. The Colonel and his officers stood listening to the music, and presently the soldiers broke into the wild 'chanson des zouaves' of the —th zouaves. It was the strangest of sights to watch that throng of dusky merry faces under their red fezes against the background of sunless northern sea. When the music was over someone with a Kodak suggested 'a group': we struck a collective attitude on one of the hotel terraces, and just as the camera was being aimed at us the Colonel turned and drew into the foreground a little grinning pock-marked soldier. 'He's just been decorated – he's got to be in the group.' A general exclamation of assent from the other officers, and a protest from the hero: 'Me? Why, my ugly mug will smash the plate!' But it didn't.

Reluctantly we turned from this interval in the day's sad round, and took the road to La Panne. Dust, dunes, deserted villages: my memory keeps no more definite vision of the run. But at sunset we came on a big seaside colony stretched out above the longest beach I ever saw:

along the sea-front, an esplanade bordered by the usual foolish villas, and behind it a single street filled with hotels and shops. All the life of the desert region we had traversed seemed to have taken refuge at La Panne. The long street was swarming with throngs of dark-uniformed Belgian soldiers, every shop seemed to be doing a thriving trade, and the hotels looked as full as beehives.

June 23rd LA PANNE.

The particular hive that has taken us in is at the extreme end of the esplanade, where asphalt and iron railings lapse abruptly into sand and sea-grass. When I looked out of my window this morning I saw only the endless stretch of brown sand against the grey roll of the Northern Ocean and, on a crest of the dunes, the figure of a solitary sentinel. But presently there was a sound of martial music, and long lines of troops came marching along the esplanade and down to the beach. The sands stretched away to east and west, a great 'field of Mars' on which an army could have manoeuvred; and the morning exercises of cavalry and infantry began. Against the brown beach the regiments in their dark uniforms looked as black as silhouettes; and the cavalry galloping by in single file suggested a black frieze of warriors encircling the dun-coloured flanks of an Etruscan vase. For hours these long-drawn-out movements of troops went on, to the wail of bugles, and under the eye of the lonely sentinel on the sandcrest; then the soldiers poured back into the town, and La Panne was once more a busy common-place *bain-de-mer*. The common-placeness, however, was only on the surface; for as one walked along the esplanade one discovered that the town had become a citadel, and that all the doll's-house villas with their silly gables and sillier names – 'Seaweed', 'The Sea-gull', 'Mon Repos', and the rest – were really a continuous line of barracks swarming with Belgian troops. In the main street there were hundreds of soldiers, pottering along in couples, chatting in groups, romping and wrestling like a crowd of school-boys, or bargaining in the shops for shell-work souvenirs and sets of post-cards; and between the dark-green and crimson uniforms was a frequent sprinkling of khaki, with the occasional pale blue of a French officer's tunic.

Before luncheon we motored over to Dunkerque. The road runs along the canal, between grass-flats and prosperous villages. No signs of war were noticeable except on the road, which was crowded with motor vans, ambulances and troops. The walls and gates of Dunkerque rose before us as calm and undisturbed as when we entered the town the day before yesterday. But within the gates we were in a desert. The bombardment had ceased the previous evening, but a death-hush lay on the town, Every house was shuttered and the streets were empty. We drove to the Place Jean Bart, where two days ago we sat at tea in the hall of the hotel. Now there was not a whole pane of glass in the windows of the square, the doors of the hotel were closed, and every now and then someone came out carrying a basketful of plaster from fallen ceilings. The whole surface of the square was literally paved with bits of glass from the hundreds of broken windows, and at the foot of David's statue of Jean Bart, just where our motor had stood while we had tea, the siege-gun of Dixmude had scooped out a hollow as big as the crater at Nieuport.

Though not a house on the square was touched, the scene was one of unmitigated desolation. It was the first time we had seen the raw wounds of a bombardment, and the freshness of the havoc seemed to accentuate its cruelty. We wandered down the street behind the hotel to the graceful Gothic church of St. Eloi, of which one aisle had been shattered; then, turning another corner, we came on a poor *bourgeois* house that had had its whole front torn away. The squalid revelation of caved-in floors, smashed wardrobes, dangling bedsteads, heaped-up blankets, topsy-turvy chairs and stoves and wash-stands was far more painful than the sight of the wounded church. St. Eloi was draped in the dignity of martyrdom, but the poor little house reminded one of some shy humdrum person suddenly exposed in the glare of a great misfortune.

A few people stood in clusters looking up at the ruins, or strayed aimlessly about the streets. Not a loud word was heard. The air seemed heavy with the suspended breath of a great city's activities: the mournful hush of Dunkerque was even more oppressive than the death-silence of Ypres. But when we came back to the Place Jean Bart the unbreakable human spirit had begun to reassert itself. A handful of children were playing in the bottom of the crater, collecting 'specimens' of glass and splintered brick; and about its rim the market-people, quietly and as a matter of course, were setting up their wooden stalls. In a few minutes the signs of German havoc would be hidden behind stacks of crockery and household utensils, and some of the pale women we had left in mournful contemplation of the ruins would be bargaining as sharply as ever for a sauce-pan or a butter-tub. Not once but a hundred times has the attitude of the average French civilian near the front reminded me of the gallant cry of Calanthea in *The Broken Heart:* 'Let me die smiling!' I should have liked to stop and spend all I had in the market of Dunkerque...

All the afternoon we wandered about La Panne. The exercises of the troops had begun again, and the deploying of those endless black lines along the beach was a sight of the strangest beauty. The sun was veiled, and heavy surges rolled in under a northerly gale. Toward evening the sea turned to cold tints of jade and pearl and tarnished silver. Far down the beach a mysterious fleet of fishing boats was drawn up on the sand, with black sails bellying in the wind; and the black riders galloping by might have landed from them, and been riding into the sunset out of some wild northern legend. Presently a knot of buglers took up their stand on the edge of the sea, facing inward, their feet in the surf, and began to play; and their call was like the call of Roland's horn, when he blew it down the pass against the heathen. On the sandcrest below my window the lonely sentinel still watched...

June 24th.

It is like coming down from the mountains to leave the front. I never had the feeling more strongly than when we passed out of Belgium this afternoon. I had it most strongly as we drove by a cluster of villas standing apart in a sterile region of sea-grass and sand. In one of those villas for nearly a year, two hearts at the highest pitch of human constancy have held up a light to the world. It is impossible to pass that house without a sense of awe. Because of the light that comes from it, dead faiths have come to life, weak convictions have grown strong, fiery impulses have turned to long endurance, and long endurance has kept the fire of impulse. In the harbour of New York there is a pompous statue of a goddess with a torch, designated as 'Liberty enlightening the World'. It seems as though the title on her pedestal might well, for the time, be transferred to the lintel of that villa in the dunes.

On leaving St. Omer we took a short cut southward across rolling country. It was a happy accident that caused us to leave the main road, for presently, over the crest of a hill, we saw surging toward us a mighty movement of British and Indian troops. A great bath of silver sunlight lay on the wheat-fields, the clumps of woodland and the hilly blue horizon, and in that slanting radiance the cavalry rode toward us, regiment after regiment of slim turbaned Indians, with delicate proud faces like the faces of Princes in Persian miniatures. Then came a long train of artillery; splendid horses, clattering gun-carriages, clear-faced English youths galloping by all aglow in the sunset. The stream of them seemed never-ending. Now and then it was checked by a train of ambulances and supply-waggons, or caught and congested in the crooked streets of a village where children and girls had come out with bunches of flowers, and bakers were selling hot loaves to the sutlers; and when we had extricated our motor from the crowd, and climbed another hill, we came on another cavalcade surging toward us through the wheat-fields. For over an hour the procession poured by, so like and yet so unlike the French division we had met on the move as we went north a few days ago; so that we seemed to have passed to the northern front, and away from it again, through a great flashing gateway in the long wall of armies guarding the civilized world from the North Sea to the Vosges.

IN ALSACE

August 13th, 1915.

My trip to the east began by a dash toward the north. Near Rheims is a little town – hardly more than a village, but in English we have no intermediate terms such as 'bourg' and 'petit bourg' – where one of the new Red Cross sanitary motor units was to be seen 'in action'. The inspection over, we climbed to a vineyard above the town and looked down at a river valley traversed by a double line of trees. The first line marked the canal, which is held by the French, who have gun-boats on it. Behind this ran the high-road, with the first-line French trenches, and just above, on the opposite slope, were the German lines. The soil being chalky, the German positions were clearly marked by two parallel white scorings across the brown hill-front; and while we watched we heard desultory firing, and saw, here and there along the ridge, the smoke-puff of an exploding shell. It was incredibly strange to stand there, among the vines humming with summer insects, and to look out over a peaceful country heavy with the coming vintage, knowing that the trees at our feet hid a line of gun-boats that were crashing death into those two white scorings on the hill.

Rheims itself brings one nearer to the war by its look of deathlike desolation. The paralysis of the bombarded towns is one of the most tragic results of the invasion. One's soul revolts at this senseless disorganizing of innumerable useful activities. Compared with the towns of the north, Rheims is relatively unharmed; but for that very reason the arrest of life seems the more futile and cruel. The Cathedral square was deserted, all the houses around it were closed. And there, before us, rose the Cathedral – *a* cathedral, rather, for it was not the one we had always known. It was, in fact, not like any cathedral on earth. When the German bombardment began, the west front of Rheims was covered with scaffolding: the shells set it on fire, and the whole church was wrapped in flames. Now the scaffolding is gone, and in the dull provincial square there stands a structure so strange and beautiful that one must search the Inferno, or some tale of Eastern magic, for words to picture the luminous unearthly vision. The lower part of the front has been warmed to deep tints of umber and burnt siena. This rich burnishing passes, higher up, through yellowish-pink and carmine, to a sulphur whitening to ivory; and the recesses of the portals and the hollows behind the statues are lined with a black denser and more velvety than any effect of shadow to be obtained by sculptured relief. The interweaving of colour over the whole blunted bruised surface recalls the metallic tints, the peacock-and-pigeon iridescences, the incredible mingling of red, blue, umber and yellow of the rocks along the Gulf of AEgina. And the wonder of the impression is increased by the sense of its evanescence; the knowledge that this

The destruction of the cathedral at Rheims.

is the beauty of disease and death, that every one of the transfigured statues must crumble under the autumn rains, that every one of the pink or golden stones is already eaten away to the core, that the Cathedral of Rheims is glowing and dying before us like a sunset...

August 14th.

A stone and brick chateau in a flat park with a stream running through it. Pampas-grass, geraniums, rustic bridges, winding paths: how *bourgeois* and sleepy it would all seem but for the sentinel challenging our motor at the gate!

Before the door a collie dozing in the sun, and a group of staff-officers waiting for luncheon. Indoors, a room with handsome tapestries, some good furniture and a table spread with the usual military maps and aeroplane-photographs. At luncheon, the General, the chiefs of the staff – a dozen in all – an officer from the General Head-quarters. The usual atmosphere of *camaraderie*, confidence, good-humour, and a kind of cheerful seriousness that I have come to regard as characteristic of the men immersed in the actual facts of the war. I set down this impression as typical of many such luncheon hours along the front...

August 15th.

This morning we set out for reconquered Alsace. For reasons unexplained to the civilian this corner of old-new France has hitherto been inaccessible, even to highly placed French officials; and there was a special sense of excitement in taking the road that led to it.

We slipped through a valley or two, passed some placid villages with vine-covered gables, and noticed that most of the signs over the shops were German. We had crossed the old frontier unawares, and were presently in the charming town of Massevaux. It was the Feast of the Assumption, and mass was just over when we reached the square before the church. The streets were full of holiday people, well-dressed, smiling, seemingly unconscious of the war. Down the church-steps, guided by fond mammas, came little girls in white dresses, with white wreaths in their hair, and carrying, in baskets slung over their shoulders, woolly lambs or blue and white Virgins. Groups of cavalry officers stood chatting with civilians in their Sunday best, and through the windows of the Golden Eagle we saw active preparations for a crowded mid-day dinner. It was all as happy and parochial as a 'Hansi' picture, and the fine old gabled houses and clean cobblestone streets made the traditional setting for an Alsacian holiday.

At the Golden Eagle we laid in a store of provisions, and started out across the mountains in the direction of Thann. The Vosges, at this season, are in their short midsummer beauty, rustling with streams, dripping with showers, balmy with the smell of firs and bracken, and of purple thyme on hot banks. We reached the top of a ridge, and, hiding the motor behind a skirt of trees, went out into the open to lunch on a sunny slope. Facing us across the valley was a tall conical hill clothed with forest. That hill was Hartmannswillerkopf, the centre of a long contest in which the French have lately been victorious; and all about us stood other crests and ridges from which German guns still look down on the valley of Thann.

Thann itself is at the valley-head, in a neck between hills; a handsome old town, with the air of prosperous stability so oddly characteristic of this tormented region. As we drove through the main street the pall of war-sadness fell on us again, darkening the light and chilling the summer air. Thann is raked by the German lines, and its windows are mostly shuttered and its streets deserted. One or two houses in the Cathedral square have been gutted, but the somewhat over-pinnacled and statued cathedral which is the pride of Thann is almost untouched, and when we entered it vespers were being sung, and a few people – mostly in black – knelt in the nave.

No greater contrast could be imagined to the happy feast-day scene we had left, a few miles off, at Massevaux; but Thann, in spite of its empty streets, is not a deserted city. A vigorous life beats in it, ready to break forth as soon as the German guns are silenced. The French administration, working on the best of terms with the population, are keeping up the civil activities of the town as the Canons of the Cathedral are continuing the rites of the Church. Many inhabitants still remain behind their closed shutters and dive down into their cellars when the shells begin to crash; and the schools, transferred to a neighbouring village, number over two thousand pupils. We walked through the town, visited a vast catacomb of a wine-cellar fitted up partly as an ambulance and partly as a shelter for the cellarless, and saw the lamentable remains of the industrial quarter along the river, which has been the special target of the German guns. Thann has been industrially ruined, all its mills are wrecked; but unlike the towns of the north it has had the good fortune to preserve its outline, its civic personality, a face that its children, when they come back, can recognize and take comfort in.

After our visit to the ruins, a diversion was suggested by the amiable administrators of Thann who had guided our sight-seeing. They were just off for a military tournament which the —th dragoons were giving that afternoon in a neighboring valley, and we were invited to go with them.

The scene of the entertainment was a meadow enclosed in an amphitheatre of rocks, with grassy ledges projecting from the cliff like tiers of opera-boxes. These points of vantage were partly occupied by interested spectators and partly by ruminating cattle; on the lowest slope, the rank and fashion of the neighbourhood was ranged on a semi-circle of chairs, and below, in the meadow, a lively steeple-chase was going on. The riding was extremely pretty, as French military riding always is. Few of the mounts were thoroughbreds – the greater number, in fact, being local cart-horses barely broken to the saddle – but their agility and dash did the greater credit to their riders. The lancers, in particular, executed an effective 'musical ride' about a central pennon, to the immense satisfaction of the fashionable public in the foreground and of the gallery on the rocks.

The audience was even more interesting than the artists. Chatting with the ladies in the front row were the General of division and his staff, groups of officers invited from the adjoining Head-quarters, and most of the civil and military administrators of the restored 'Departement du Haut Rhin'. All classes had turned out in honour of the fete, and everyone was in a holiday mood. The people among whom we sat were mostly Alsatian property-owners, many of them industrials of Thann. Some had been driven from their homes, others had seen their mills destroyed, all had been living for a year on the perilous edge of war, under the menace of reprisals too hideous to picture; yet the humour prevailing was that of any group of merry-makers in a peaceful garrison town. I have seen nothing, in my wanderings along the front, more indicative of the good-breeding of the French than the spirit of the ladies and gentlemen who sat chatting with the officers on that grassy slope of Alsace.

The display of *haute ecole* was to be followed by an exhibition of 'transportation throughout the ages', headed by a Gaulish chariot driven by a trooper with a long horsehair moustache and mistletoe wreath, and ending in a motor of which the engine had been taken out and replaced by a large placid white horse. Unluckily a heavy rain began while this instructive 'number' awaited its turn, and we had to leave before Vercingetorix had led his warriors into the ring...

August 16th.

Up and up into the mountains. We started early, taking our way along a narrow interminable valley that sloped up gradually toward the east. The road was encumbered with a stream of hooded supply vans drawn by mules, for we were on the way to one of the main positions in the Vosges, and this train of provisions is kept up day and night. Finally we reached a mountain village under fir-clad slopes, with a cold stream rushing down from the hills. On one side of the road was a rustic inn, on the other, among the firs, a chalet occupied by the brigade

Head-quarters. Everywhere about us swarmed the little 'chasseurs Alpins' in blue Tam o'Shanters and leather gaiters. For a year we had been reading of these heroes of the hills, and here we were among them, looking into their thin weather-beaten faces and meeting the twinkle of their friendly eyes. Very friendly they all were, and yet, for Frenchmen, inarticulate and shy. All over the world, no doubt, the mountain silences breed this kind of reserve, this shrinking from the glibness of the valleys. Yet one had fancied that French fluency must soar as high as Mont Blanc.

Mules were brought, and we started on a long ride up the mountain. The way led first over open ledges, with deep views into valleys blue with distance, then through miles of forest, first of beech and fir, and finally all of fir. Above the road the wooded slopes rose interminably and here and there we came on tiers of mules, three or four hundred together, stabled under the trees, in stalls dug out of different levels of the slope. Nearby were shelters for the men, and perhaps at the next bend a village of 'trappers' huts', as the officers call the log-cabins they build in this region. These colonies are always bustling with life: men busy cleaning their arms, hauling material for new cabins, washing or mending their clothes, or carrying down the mountain from the camp-kitchen the two-handled pails full of steaming soup. The kitchen is always in the most protected quarter of the camp, and generally at some distance in the rear. Other soldiers, their job over, are lolling about in groups, smoking, gossiping or writing home, the 'Soldiers' Letter-pad' propped on a patched blue knee, a scarred fist laboriously driving the fountain pen received in hospital. Some are leaning over the shoulder of a pal who has just received a Paris paper, others chuckling together at the jokes of their own French journal – the *Echo du Ravin*, the *Journal des Poilus*, or the *Diable Bleu*: little papers ground out in purplish script on foolscap, and adorned with comic-sketches and a wealth of local humour.

Higher up, under a fir-belt, at the edge of a meadow, the officer who rode ahead signed to us to dismount and scramble after him. We plunged under the trees, into what seemed a thicker thicket, and found it to be a thatch of branches woven to screen the muzzles of a battery. The big guns were all about us, crouched in these sylvan lairs like wild beasts waiting to spring; and near each gun hovered its attendant gunner, proud, possessive, important as a bridegroom with his bride.

We climbed and climbed again, reaching at last a sun-and-wind-burnt common which forms the top of one of the highest mountains in the region. The forest was left below us and only a belt of dwarf firs ran along the edge of the great grassy shoulder. We dismounted, the mules were tethered among the trees, and our guide led us to an insignificant looking stone in the grass. On one face of the stone was cut the letter F., on the other was a D.; we stood on what, till a year ago, was the boundary line between Republic and Empire. Since then, in certain places, the line has been bent back a long way; but where we stood we were still under German guns, and we had to creep along in the shelter of the squat firs to reach the outlook on the edge of the plateau. From there, under a sky of racing clouds, we saw outstretched below us the Promised Land of Alsace. On one horizon, far off in the plain, gleamed the roofs and spires of Colmar, on the other rose the purplish heights beyond the Rhine. Nearby stood a ring of bare hills, those closest to us scarred by ridges of upheaved earth, as if giant moles had been zigzagging over them; and just under us, in a little green valley, lay the roofs of a peaceful village. The earth-ridges and the peaceful village were still German; but the French positions went down the mountain, almost to the valley's edge; and one dark peak on the right was already French.

We stopped at a gap in the firs and walked to the brink of the plateau. Just under us lay a rock-rimmed lake. More zig-zag earthworks surmounted it on all sides, and on the nearest shore was the branched roofing of another great mule-shelter. We were looking down at the spot to which the night-caravans of the Chasseurs Alpins descend to distribute supplies to the fighting line.

'Who goes there? Attention! You're in sight of the lines!' a voice called out from the firs, and our companion signed to us to move back. We had been rather too conspicuously facing the German batteries on the opposite slope, and our presence might have drawn their fire on an artillery observation post installed nearby. We retreated hurriedly and unpacked our luncheon-basket on the more sheltered side of the ridge. As we sat there in the grass, swept by a great mountain breeze full of the scent of thyme and myrtle, while the flutter of birds, the hum of insects, the still

A Mitrailleuse detachment.

and busy life of the hills went on all about us in the sunshine, the pressure of the encircling line of death grew more intolerably real. It is not in the mud and jokes and every-day activities of the trenches that one most feels the damnable insanity of war; it is where it lurks like a mythical monster in scenes to which the mind has always turned for rest.

We had not yet made the whole tour of the mountaintop; and after luncheon we rode over to a point where a long narrow yoke connects it with a spur projecting directly above the German lines. We left our mules in hiding and walked along the yoke, a mere knife-edge of rock rimmed with dwarf vegetation. Suddenly we heard an explosion behind us: one of the batteries we had passed on the way up was giving tongue. The German lines roared back and for twenty minutes the exchange of invective thundered on. The firing was almost incessant; it seemed as if a great arch of steel were being built up above us in the crystal air. And we could follow each curve of sound from its incipience to its final crash in the trenches. There were four distinct phases: the sharp bang from the cannon, the long furious howl overhead, the dispersed and spreading noise of the shell's explosion, and then the roll of its reverberation from cliff to cliff. This is what we heard as we crouched in the lee of the firs: what we saw when we looked out between them was only an occasional burst of white smoke and red flame from one hillside, and on the opposite one, a minute later, a brown geyser of dust.

Presently a deluge of rain descended on us, driving us back to our mules, and down the nearest mountain-trail through rivers of mud. It rained all the way: rained in such floods and cataracts that the very rocks of the mountain seemed to dissolve and turn into mud. As we slid down through it we met strings of Chasseurs Alpins coming up, splashed to the waist with wet red clay, and leading pack-mules so coated with it that they looked like studio models from which the sculptor has just pulled off the dripping sheet. Lower down we came on more 'trapper' settlements, so saturated and reeking with wet that they gave us a glimpse of what the winter months on the front must be. No more cheerful polishing of fire-arms, hauling of faggots, chatting and smoking in sociable groups: everybody had crept under the doubtful shelter of branches and tarpaulins; the whole army was back in its burrows.

August 17th.

Sunshine again for our arrival at Belfort. The invincible city lies unpretentiously behind its green glacis and escutcheoned gates; but the guardian Lion under the Citadel – well, the Lion is figuratively as well as literally *a la hauteur*. With the sunset flush on him, as he crouched aloft in his red lair below the fort, he might almost have claimed kin with his mighty prototypes of the Assarbanipal frieze. One wondered a little, seeing whose work he was; but probably it is easier for an artist to symbolize an heroic town than the abstract and elusive divinity who sheds light on the world from New York harbour.

From Belfort back into reconquered Alsace the road runs through a gentle landscape of fields and orchards. We were bound for Dannemarie, one of the towns of the plain, and a centre of the new administration. It is the usual 'gros bourg' of Alsace, with comfortable old houses in espaliered gardens: dull, well-to-do, contented; not in the least the kind of setting demanded by the patriotism which has to be fed on pictures of little girls singing the Marseillaise in Alsatian head-dresses and old men with operatic waistcoats tottering forward to kiss the flag. What we saw at Dannemarie was less conspicuous to the eye but much more nourishing to the imagination. The military and civil administrators had the kindness and patience to explain their work and show us something of its results; and the visit left one with the impression of a slow and quiet process of adaptation wisely planned and fruitfully carried out. We *did*, in fact, hear the school-girls of Dannemarie sing the Marseillaise – and the boys too – but, what was far more interesting, we saw them studying under the direction of the teachers who had always had them in charge, and found that everywhere it had been the aim of the French officials to let the routine of the village policy go on undisturbed. The German signs remain over the shop-fronts except where the shop-keepers have chosen to paint them out; as is happening more and more frequently. When a functionary has to be replaced he is chosen from the same town or the same district, and even the *personnel* of the civil and military administration is mainly composed of officers and civilians of Alsatian stock. The heads of both these departments, who accompanied us on our rounds, could talk to the children and old people in German as well as in their local dialect; and, as far as a passing observer could discern, it seemed as though everything had been done to reduce to a minimum the sense of strangeness and friction which is inevitable in the transition from one rule to another. The interesting point was that this exercise of tact and tolerance seemed to proceed not from any pressure of expediency but from a sympathetic understanding of the point of view of this people of the border. I heard in Dannemarie not a syllable of lyrical patriotism or post-card sentimentality, but only a kindly and impartial estimate of facts as they were and must be dealt with.

August 18th.

Today again we started early for the mountains. Our road ran more to the westward, through the heart of the Vosges, and up to a fold of the hills near the borders of Lorraine. We stopped at a Head-quarters where a young officer of dragoons was to join us, and learned from him that we were to be allowed to visit some of the first-line trenches which we had looked out on from a high-perched observation post on our former visit to the Vosges. Violent fighting was going on in that particular region, and after a climb of an hour or two we had to leave the motor at a sheltered angle of the road and strike across the hills on foot. Our path lay through the forest, and every now and then we caught a glimpse of the high-road running below us in full

Poster drumming up support for the Alsace-Lorraine region.

view of the German batteries. Presently we reached a point where the road was screened by a thick growth of trees behind which an observation post had been set up. We scrambled down and looked through the peephole. Just below us lay a valley with a village in its centre, and to the left and right of the village were two hills, the one scored with French, the other with German trenches. The village, at first sight, looked as normal as those through which we had been passing; but a closer inspection showed that its steeple was shattered and that some of its houses were unroofed. Part of it was held by German, part by French troops. The cemetery adjoining the church, and a quarry just under it, belonged to the Germans; but a line of French trenches ran from the farther side of the church up to the French batteries on the right hand hill. Parallel with this line, but starting from the other side of the village, was a hollow lane leading up to a single tree. This lane was a German trench, protected by the guns of the left hand hill; and between the two lay perhaps fifty yards of ground. All this was close under us; and closer still was a slope of open ground leading up to the village and traversed by a rough cart-track. Along this track in the hot sunshine little French soldiers, the size of tin toys, were scrambling up with bags and loads of faggots, their ant-like activity as orderly and untroubled as if the two armies had not lain trench to trench a few yards away. It was one of those strange and contradictory scenes of war that bring home to the bewildered looker-on the utter impossibility of picturing how the thing *really happens.*

While we stood watching we heard the sudden scream of a battery close above us. The crest of the hill we were climbing was alive with 'Seventy-fives', and the piercing noise seemed to burst out at our very backs. It was the most terrible war-shriek I had heard: a kind of wolfish baying that called up an image of all the dogs of war simultaneously tugging at their leashes. There is a dreadful majesty in the sound of a distant cannonade; but these yelps and hisses roused only thoughts of horror. And there, on the opposite slope, the black and brown geysers were beginning to spout up from the German trenches; and from the batteries above them came the puff and roar of retaliation. Below us, along the cart-track, the little French soldiers continued to scramble up peacefully to the dilapidated village; and presently a group of officers of dragoons, emerging from the wood, came down to welcome us to their Head-quarters.

We continued to climb through the forest, the cannonade still whistling overhead, till we reached the most elaborate trapper colony we had yet seen. Half underground, walled with logs, and deeply roofed by sods tufted with ferns and moss, the cabins were scattered under the trees and connected with each other by paths bordered with white stones. Before the Colonel's cabin the soldiers had made a banked-up flower-bed sown with annuals; and farther up the slope stood a log chapel, a mere gable with a wooden altar under it, all tapestried with ivy and holly. Nearby was the chaplain's subterranean dwelling. It was reached by a deep cutting with ivy-covered sides, and ivy and fir-boughs masked the front. This sylvan retreat had just been completed, and the officers, the chaplain, and the soldiers loitering nearby, were all equally eager to have it seen and hear it praised.

The commanding officer, having done the honours of the camp, led us about a quarter of a mile down the hillside to an open cutting which marked the beginning of the trenches. From the cutting we passed into a long tortuous burrow walled and roofed with carefully fitted logs. The earth floor was covered by a sort of wooden lattice. The only light entering this tunnel was a faint ray from an occasional narrow slit screened by branches; and beside each of these peep-holes hung a shield-shaped metal shutter to be pushed over it in case of emergency.

The passage wound down the hill, almost doubling on itself, in order to give a view of all the surrounding lines. Presently the roof became much higher, and we saw on one side a curtained niche about five feet above the floor. One of the officers pulled the curtain back, and there, on a narrow shelf, a gun between his knees, sat a dragoon, his eyes on a peep-hole. The curtain was hastily drawn again behind his motionless figure, lest the faint light at his back should betray him. We passed by several of these helmeted watchers, and now and then we came to a deeper recess in which a mitrailleuse squatted, its black nose thrust through a net of branches. Sometimes the roof of the tunnel was so low that we had to bend nearly double; and at intervals we came to heavy doors, made of logs and sheeted with iron, which shut off one section from another. It is hard to guess the distance one covers in creeping through an unlit passage with different levels and countless turnings; but we must have descended the hillside for at least a mile before we came out into a half-ruined farmhouse. This building, which had kept nothing but its outer walls and one or two partitions between the rooms, had been transformed into an observation post. In each of its corners a ladder led up to a little shelf on the level of what was once the second story, and on the shelf sat a dragoon at his peep-hole. Below, in the dilapidated rooms, the usual life of a camp was going on. Some of the soldiers were playing cards at a kitchen table, others mending their clothes, or writing letters or chuckling together (not too loud) over a comic newspaper. It might have been a scene anywhere along the second-line trenches but for the lowered voices, the suddenness with which I was drawn back from a slit in the wall through which I had incautiously peered, and the presence of these helmeted watchers overhead.

We plunged underground again and began to descend through another darker and narrower tunnel. In the upper one there had been one or two roofless stretches where one could straighten one's back and breathe; but here we were in pitch blackness, and saved from breaking our necks only by the gleam of the pocket-light which the young lieutenant who led the party shed on our path. As he whisked it up and down to warn us of sudden steps or sharp corners he remarked that at night even this faint glimmer was forbidden, and that it was a bad job going back and forth from the last outpost till one had learned the turnings.

The last outpost was a half-ruined farmhouse like the other. A telephone connected it with Head-quarters and more dumb dragoons sat motionless on their lofty shelves. The house was shut off from the tunnel by an armoured door, and the orders were that in case of attack that door should be barred from within and the access to the tunnel defended to the death by the men in the outpost. We were on the extreme verge of the defences, on a slope just above the village over which we had heard the artillery roaring a few hours earlier. The spot where we stood was raked on all sides by the enemy's lines, and the nearest trenches were only a few yards away. But of all this nothing was really perceptible or comprehensible to me. As far as my own observation went, we might have been a hundred miles from the valley we had looked down on, where the French soldiers were walking peacefully up the cart-track in the sunshine. I only knew that we had come out of a black labyrinth into a gutted house among fruit-trees, where soldiers were lounging and smoking, and people whispered as they do about a death-bed. Over a break in the walls I saw another gutted farmhouse close by in another orchard: it was an enemy outpost, and silent watchers in helmets of another shape sat there watching on the same high shelves. But all this was infinitely less real and terrible than the cannonade above the disputed village. The artillery had ceased and the air was full of summer murmurs. Close by on a sheltered ledge I saw a patch of vineyard with dewy cobwebs hanging to the vines. I could not understand where we were, or what it was all about, or why a shell from the enemy outpost did not suddenly annihilate us. And then, little by little, there came over me the sense of that mute reciprocal watching from trench to trench: the interlocked stare of innumerable pairs of eyes, stretching on, mile after mile, along the whole sleepless line from Dunkerque to Belfort.

My last vision of the French front which I had traveled from end to end was this picture of a shelled house where a few men, who sat smoking and playing cards in the sunshine, had orders to hold out to the death rather than let their fraction of that front be broken.

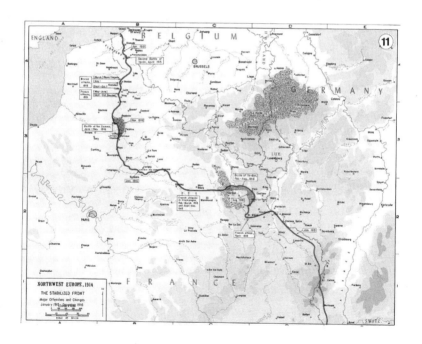

The Western Front in 1914, from Dunkerque to Belfort.

THE TONE OF FRANCE

Nobody now asks the question that so often, at the beginning of the war, came to me from the other side of the world: '*What is France like?*' Everyone knows what France has proved to be like: from being a difficult problem she has long since become a luminous instance.

Nevertheless, to those on whom that illumination has shone only from far off, there may still be something to learn about its component elements; for it has come to consist of many separate rays, and the weary strain of the last year has been the spectroscope to decompose them. From the very beginning, when one felt the effulgence as the mere pale brightness before dawn, the attempt to define it was irresistible. 'There *is* a tone –' the tingling sense of it was in the air from the first days, the first hours – 'but what does it consist in? And just how is one aware of it?' In those days the answer was comparatively easy. The tone of France after the declaration of war was the white glow of dedication: a great nation's collective impulse (since there is no English equivalent for that winged word, *élan*) to resist destruction. But at that time no one knew what the resistance was to cost, how long it would have to last, what sacrifices, material and moral, it would necessitate. And for the moment baser sentiments were silenced: greed, self-interest, pusillanimity seemed to have been purged from the race. The great sitting of the Chamber, that almost religious celebration of defensive union, really expressed the opinion of the whole people. It is fairly easy to soar to the empyrean when one is carried on the wings of such an impulse, and when one does not know how long one is to be kept suspended at the breathing-limit.

But there is a term to the flight of the most soaring *élan*. It is likely, after a while, to come back broken-winged and resign itself to barn-yard bounds. National judgments cannot remain for long above individual feelings; and you cannot get a national 'tone' out of anything less than a whole nation. The really interesting thing, therefore, was to see, as the war went on, and grew into a calamity unheard of in human annals, how the French spirit would meet it, and what virtues extract from it.

The war has been a calamity unheard of; but France has never been afraid of the unheard of. No race has ever yet so audaciously dispensed with old precedents; as none has ever so revered their relics. It is a great strength to be able to walk without the support of analogies; and France has always shown that strength in times of crisis. The absorbing question, as the war went on, was to discover how far down into the people this intellectual audacity penetrated, how instinctive it had become, and how it would endure the strain of prolonged inaction.

There was never much doubt about the army. When a warlike race has an invader on its soil, the men holding back the invader can never be said to be inactive. But behind the army were the waiting millions to whom that long motionless line in the trenches might gradually have become a mere condition of thought, an accepted limitation to all sorts of activities and pleasures. The danger was that such a war – static, dogged, uneventful – might gradually cramp instead of enlarging the mood of the lookers-on. Conscription, of course, was there to minimize this danger. Everyone was sharing alike in the glory and the woe. But the glory was not of a kind to penetrate or dazzle. It requires more imagination to see the halo around tenacity than around dash; and the French still cling to the view that they are, so to speak, the patentees and proprietors of dash, and much less at home with his dull drudge of a partner. So there was reason to fear, in the long run, a gradual but irresistible disintegration, not of public opinion, but of something subtler and more fundamental: public sentiment. It was possible that civilian France, while collectively seeming to remain at the same height, might individually deteriorate and diminish in its attitude toward the war.

The French would not be human, and therefore would not be interesting, if one had not perceived in them occasional symptoms of such a peril. There has not been a Frenchman or a Frenchwoman – save a few harmless and perhaps nervous theorizers – who has wavered about the military policy of the country; but there have naturally been some who have found it less easy than they could have foreseen to live up to the sacrifices it has necessitated. Of course there have been such people: one would have had to postulate them if they had not come within one's experience. There have been some to whom it was harder than they imagined to give up a certain way of living, or a certain kind of breakfast-roll; though the French, being fundamentally temperate, are far less the slaves of the luxuries they have invented than are the other races who have adopted these luxuries.

There have been many more who found the sacrifice of personal happiness – of all that made life livable, or one's country worth fighting for – infinitely harder than the most apprehensive imagination could have pictured. There have been mothers and widows for whom a single grave, or the appearance of one name on the missing list, has turned the whole conflict into an idiot's tale. There have been many such; but there have apparently not been enough to deflect by a hair's breadth the subtle current of public sentiment; unless it is truer, as it is infinitely more inspiring, to suppose that, of this company of blinded baffled sufferers, almost all have had the strength to hide their despair and to say of the great national effort which has lost most of its meaning to them: 'Though it slay me, yet will I trust in it.' That is probably the finest triumph of the tone of France: that its myriad fiery currents flow from so many hearts made insensible by suffering, that so many dead hands feed its undying lamp.

This does not in the least imply that resignation is the prevailing note in the tone of France. The attitude

of the French people, after fourteen months of trial, is
not one of submission to unparalleled calamity. It is one
of exaltation, energy, the hot resolve to dominate the
disaster. In all classes the feeling is the same: every word
and every act is based on the resolute ignoring of any
alternative to victory. The French people no more think
of a compromise than people would think of facing a
flood or an earthquake with a white flag.

Two questions are likely to be put to any observer of
the struggle who risks such assertions. What, one may
be asked, are the proofs of this national tone? And what
conditions and qualities seem to minister to it?

The proofs, now that 'the tumult and the shouting
dies', and civilian life has dropped back into something
like its usual routine, are naturally less definable than
at the outset. One of the most evident is the spirit in
which all kinds of privations are accepted. No one who
has come in contact with the work-people and small
shop-keepers of Paris in the last year can fail to be
struck by the extreme dignity and grace with which
doing without things is practised. The Frenchwoman
leaning in the door of her empty *boutique* still wears
the smile with which she used to calm the impatience
of crowding shoppers. The seamstress living on the
meagre pay of a charity work-room gives her day's
sewing as faithfully as if she were working for full wages
in a fashionable *atelier*, and never tries, by the least hint
of private difficulties, to extract additional help. The
habitual cheerfulness of the Parisian workwoman rises,
in moments of sorrow, to the finest fortitude. In a work-
room where many women have been employed since

the beginning of the war, a young girl of sixteen heard late one afternoon that her only brother had been killed. She had a moment of desperate distress; but there was a big family to be helped by her small earnings, and the next morning punctually she was back at work. In this same work-room the women have one half-holiday in the week, without reduction of pay; yet if an order has to be rushed through for a hospital they give up that one afternoon as gaily as if they were doing it for their pleasure. But if anyone who has lived for the last year among the workers and small tradesmen of Paris should begin to cite instances of endurance, self-denial and secret charity, the list would have no end. The essential of it all is the spirit in which these acts are accomplished.

The second question: What are the conditions and qualities that have produced such results? is less easy to answer. The door is so largely open to conjecture that every explanation must depend largely on the answerer's personal bias. But one thing is certain. France has not achieved her present tone by the sacrifice of any of her national traits, but rather by their extreme keying up; therefore the surest way of finding a clue to that tone is to try to single out whatever distinctively 'French' characteristics – or those that appear such to the envious alien – have a direct bearing on the present attitude of France. Which (one must ask) of all their multiple gifts most help the French today to be what they are in just the way they are?

Intelligence! is the first and instantaneous answer. Many French people seem unaware of this. They are sincerely persuaded that the curbing of their critical activity has been one of the most important and useful results of the war. One is told that, in a spirit of patriotism, this fault-finding people has learned not to find fault. Nothing could be more untrue. The French, when they have a grievance, do not air it in the *Times:* their forum is the cafe and not the newspaper. But in the cafe they are talking as freely as ever, discriminating as keenly and judging as passionately. The difference is that the very exercise of their intelligence on a problem larger and more difficult than any they have hitherto faced has freed them from the dominion of most of the prejudices, catch-words and conventions that directed opinion before the war. Then their intelligence ran in fixed channels; now it has overflowed its banks.

This release has produced an immediate readjusting of all the elements of national life. In great trials a race is tested by its values; and the war has shown the world what are the real values of France. Never for an instant has this people, so expert in the great art of living, imagined that life consisted in being alive. Enamoured of pleasure and beauty, dwelling freely and frankly in the present, they have yet kept their sense of larger meanings, have understood life to be made up of many things past and to come, of renunciation as well as satisfaction, of traditions as well as experiments, of dying as much as of living. Never have they considered life as a thing to be cherished in itself, apart from its reactions and its relations.

Intelligence first, then, has helped France to be what she is; and next, perhaps, one of its corollaries, *expression*.

French wartime poster in support of the army.

The French are the first to laugh at themselves for running to words: they seem to regard their gift for expression as a weakness, a possible deterrent to action. The last year has not confirmed that view. It has rather shown that eloquence is a supplementary weapon. By 'eloquence' I naturally do not mean public speaking, nor yet the rhetorical writing too often associated with the word. Rhetoric is the dressing-up of conventional sentiment, eloquence the fearless expression of real emotion. And this gift of the fearless expression of emotion – fearless, that is, of ridicule, or of indifference in the hearer – has been an inestimable strength to France. It is a sign of the high average of French intelligence that feeling well-worded can stir and uplift it; that 'words' are not half shamefacedly regarded as something separate from, and extraneous to, emotion, or even as a mere vent for it, but as actually animating and forming it. Every additional faculty for exteriorizing states of feeling, giving them a face and a language, is a moral as well as an artistic asset, and Goethe was never wiser than when he wrote:

A god gave me the voice to speak my pain.

It is not too much to say that the French are at this moment drawing a part of their national strength from their language. The piety with which they have cherished and cultivated it has made it a precious instrument in their hands. It can say so beautifully what they feel that they find strength and renovation in using it; and the word once uttered is passed on, and carries the same help to others. Countless instances of such happy expression could be cited by anyone who has lived the last year in France. On the bodies of young soldiers have been found letters of farewell to their parents that made one think of some heroic Elizabethan verse; and the mothers robbed of these sons have sent them an answering cry of courage.

'Thank you,' such a mourner wrote me the other day, 'for having understood the cruelty of our fate, and having pitied us. Thank you also for having exalted the pride that is mingled with our unutterable sorrow.' Simply that, and no more; but she might have been speaking for all the mothers of France.

When the eloquent expression of feeling does not issue in action – or at least in a state of mind equivalent to action – it sinks to the level of rhetoric; but in France at this moment expression and conduct supplement and reflect each other. And this brings me to the other great attribute which goes to making up the tone of France: the quality of courage. It is not unintentionally that it comes last on my list. French courage is courage rationalized, courage thought out, and found necessary to some special end; it is, as much as any other quality of the French temperament, the result of French intelligence.

No people so sensitive to beauty, so penetrated with a passionate interest in life, so endowed with the power to express and immortalize that interest, can ever really enjoy destruction for its own sake. The French hate 'militarism'. It is stupid, inartistic, unimaginative and enslaving; there could not be four better French reasons for detesting it. Nor have the French ever enjoyed the

Another French poster asking for funds to support the war effort.

savage forms of sport which stimulate the blood of more apathetic or more brutal races. Neither prize-fighting nor bull-fighting is of the soil in France, and Frenchmen do not settle their private differences impromptu with their fists: they do it, logically and with deliberation, on the duelling-ground. But when a national danger threatens, they instantly become what they proudly and justly call themselves – 'a warlike nation' – and apply to the business in hand the ardour, the imagination, the perseverance that have made them for centuries the great creative force of civilization. Every French soldier knows why he is fighting, and why, at this moment, physical courage is the first quality demanded of him; every Frenchwoman knows why war is being waged, and why her moral courage is needed to supplement the soldier's contempt of death.

The women of France are supplying this moral courage in act as well as in word. Frenchwomen, as a rule, are perhaps less instinctively 'courageous', in the elementary sense, than their Anglo-Saxon sisters. They are afraid of more things, and are less ashamed of showing their fear. The French mother coddles her children, the boys as well as the girls: when they tumble and bark their knees they are expected to cry, and not taught to control themselves as English and American children are. I have seen big French boys bawling over a cut or a bruise that an Anglo-Saxon girl of the same age would have felt compelled to bear without a tear. Frenchwomen are timid for themselves as well as for their children. They are afraid of the unexpected, the unknown, the experimental. It is not part of the Frenchwoman's training to pretend to have physical courage. She has not the advantage of our discipline in the hypocrisies of 'good form' when she is called on to be brave, she must draw her courage from her brains. She must first be convinced of the necessity of heroism; after that she is fit to go bridle to bridle with Jeanne d'Arc.

The same display of reasoned courage is visible in the hasty adaptation of the Frenchwoman to all kinds of uncongenial jobs. Almost every kind of service she has been called to render since the war began has been fundamentally uncongenial. A French doctor once remarked to me that Frenchwomen never make really good sick-nurses except when they are nursing their own people. They are too personal, too emotional, and too much interested in more interesting things, to take to the fussy details of good nursing, except when it can help someone they care for. Even then, as a rule, they are not systematic or tidy; but they make up for these deficiencies by inexhaustible willingness and sympathy. And it has been easy for them to become good war-nurses, because every Frenchwoman who nurses a French soldier feels that she is caring for her kin. The French war-nurse sometimes mislays an instrument or forgets to sterilize a dressing; but she almost always finds the consoling word to say and the right tone to take with her wounded soldiers. That profound solidarity which is one of the results of conscription flowers, in war-time, in an exquisite and impartial devotion.

This, then, is what 'France is like'. The whole civilian part of the nation seems merged in one symbolic figure, carrying help and hope to the fighters or passionately bent above the wounded. The devotion, the self-denial, seem instinctive; but they are really based on a reasoned

French soldiers on the front line.

knowledge of the situation and on an unflinching estimate of values. All France knows today that real 'life' consists in the things that make it worth living, and that these things, for France, depend on the free expression of her national genius. If France perishes as an intellectual light and as a moral force every Frenchman perishes with her; and the only death that Frenchmen fear is not death in the trenches but death by the extinction of their national ideal. It is against this death that the whole nation is fighting; and it is the reasoned recognition of their peril which, at this moment, is making the most intelligent people in the world the most sublime.

THE END